DOGS
ON
SWEATERS

First published in the United States of America in 2019 by
Trafalgar Square Books
North Pomfret, Vermont 05053

Copyright © Pavilion Books Company Ltd 2018
Text and pattern copyright © Sally Muir & Joanna Osborne 2018

ISBN: 978-1-57076-934-4

Library of Congress Control Number: 2018961057

Reproduction by Colourdepth

Printed in China
10 9 8 7 6 5 4 3 2 1

DOGS ON SWEATERS

KNITTING PATTERNS FOR 18 DIFFERENT BREEDS

SALLY MUIR & JOANNA OSBORNE

Trafalgar Square
North Pomfret, Vermont

DOGS ON SWEATERS

Dogs on Sweaters combines our two great interests: dogs and knitwear. We have been knitwear designers, as Muir and Osborne, for many years, and animals have appeared in our designs right from the beginning of our business. In the early days there was the Princess Diana sheep sweater and the Wolf in Sheep's Clothing design for *Cosmopolitan* magazine. Our first knitting book was *Pet Heaven: The Animal Accessory Bible*.

We appeared on *The Martha Stewart Show*, hosting a dog fashion show and demonstrating how to upcycle a cardigan into a dog coat. Then we decided to go three-dimensional with our first *Best in Show* book, *Knit Your Own Dog*. This was a remarkable success that encouraged us to write a further six books in the series. As with our *Best in Show* books, we are hoping that you use this book as inspiration and adapt our designs to your own particular dog.

We have designed for men, women, children, babies and even dogs, so if you are a keen knitter, your whole family can now wear dogs on sweaters.

HOW TO USE THIS BOOK

MAKING THE SWEATERS

There are three adult options and three child/baby options, each with its own master pattern, so the first decision to make is to choose the shape of the sweater:

- Woman's Raglan Pullover (page 16): this is neat and boxy.
- Woman's Long and Loose Pullover (page 18): this is exactly what it is, easy to wear and suits most body shapes.
- Man's Pullover (page 20): relaxed style, set-in sleeves.
- Child's Pullover (page 68): dropped shoulders, loose shape.
- Baby's Raglan Pullover (page 70): for up to age 3 years, raglan shape, similar to a sweatshirt.
- Baby's Cardigan (page 72): for up to age 6 months, set-in sleeves, easy cardigan.

The second decision is to choose the dog you would like to knit. There is a choice of 18 dogs – plus a slogan design – for the adult sweaters (see pages 22–27), and 8 dogs for the child and baby sweaters (see pages 76–79). Start by following the master pattern for your selected sweater. When working the front of the sweater, refer to the separate instructions and chart for your chosen dog breed (see index of dog breeds on page 140).

YARNS

The adult sweaters are worked in worsted-weight yarn. We have used either Cascade 220 Solids and Heathers (CYCA #4) or Debbie Bliss Donegal Luxury Tweed Aran (CYCA #4) yarn for the main sweater. The yarn quantities for the main color are listed in the master patterns. For the dogs we have used mainly Cascade 220 because of

the superb color range. The yarn requirements for each dog are listed with the dog breed.

For the child and baby knitwear, we recommend Erika Knight's British Blue Wool (CYCA #3) or British Blue 100 (CYCA #3). This lovely soft, airy yarn is available at most yarn stores as well as online, but any double-knit (DK) weight would do.

DESIGN CHOICES

Our patterns are designed to be used as a template, to which you can then add details. There are two options for the rib: work in one color throughout, or add a contrast edge to the back, front and sleeves. Both possibilities are included in the master patterns. The dog chart pattern can be started anywhere on the sweater. We have generally placed the dog in the middle of the front, slightly higher than the center.

All of the dogs can be knitted directly onto the main color of the sweater, or they can be framed inside a square or oval in a contrasting color. The only exception is the Dachshund, which can be knitted onto a contrasting stripe running the full width of the sweater to accommodate its length.

A contrast square is much easier to work than an oval. We suggest knitting about 4 rows of contrast color above and below the dog, and 3 contrast stitches on either side of the dog. For the oval, use graph paper to draw an oval around the dog, leaving about 3 stitches/4 rows between the dog's nose/tail and the edge of the oval.

LETTERING

We have included an alphabet for dog names and dog slogans (page 130). Follow the pattern for the Golden Retriever front for the positioning of a dog's name (page 40); the height of the lettering will remain the same, but the width of the name will vary. Using the alphabet provided, copy your dog's name onto graph paper and adjust the position as follows for a slogan sweater.

For slogan sweaters, copy the chosen letters onto graph paper, then count the stitches and rows. To position the slogan, refer to the index of dogs (page 140) and select the dog that is closest in size to your slogan. To center the slogan, count the number of stitches, subtract these from the width of the sweater and divide by two. Use a small ball of contrast color for each letter, and take the main color across the back of the letter. If there are more than 3 stitches in the contrast color, weave the main color across the back of the letter using the Fair Isle method (see below).

INTARSIA METHOD

We recommend using the intarsia method for knitting the dogs, although you can take the main color across the back of skinny legs, such as those of the Whippet. Use a small ball of yarn for each area of color, otherwise the yarns will easily become tangled. When changing to a new color, twist the yarns on the wrong side of the work to prevent holes from forming. When starting a new row, turn the knitting so that the yarns are hanging from it, untwisting them as much as possible. If you have several colors, you may occasionally have to reorganize the yarns at the back of the knitting.

FAIR ISLE METHOD

Use this method for skinny legs, Dalmatian spots and lettering. Begin knitting with the first color, then drop this when you introduce the second color. When you come to the first color again, take it under the second color to twist the yarns. When you come to the second color again, take it over the first color. If working over more than 3 stitches of the second color, catch the first color at the back of the work with the second color so that the first color strand is not floating loose. The secret is not to pull the strands on the wrong side of the work too tightly or the work will pucker.

EMBROIDERY STITCHES

Some of the dogs have a single stitch in a contrast color for the eyes or nose. Rather than knitting this as part of the pattern, you can use the contrast color to make a duplicate stitch over the knitted stitch below.

French knots are used to make the eyes of many of the dogs. You can make the knots smaller or larger, as you wish.

DUPLICATE STITCH

Thread a tapestry needle with yarn and insert it through the knitting from back to front, bringing it out at the bottom of the "V" of the required stitch. Insert the needle from right to left under the two strands of yarn at the base of the stitch above, then take it back through the entry point. This makes a duplicate stitch over the original stitch. YouTube is a helpful source for tutorials if you need extra assistance.

FRENCH KNOTS

Thread a tapestry needle with yarn and insert it through the knitting from back to front. Wrap the yarn around the needle about three times, depending on the thickness of the yarn and how big you want the finished knot to be. To finish the knot, insert the needle back into the knitting no more than one stitch away from where you came out. Slowly pull the needle and ease the yarn through the wrapped loops to complete a French knot.

CHECKLIST
- Shape of sweater
- Dog breed
- Contrast edges or not
- Square, oval, stripe or dog only
- Lettering

KNIT YOUR OWN DOG

Feel free to play around with colors and markings, with the position of the dog on the sweater and with the shape of the background – square, oval or stripe. Among the charts at the back of the book we have included an alphabet, so you can make up your own dog-related phrases, or add your dog's name or initials. These can also be added to the baby blanket if you want to personalize it. Here are our tips for knitting your own dog sweater.

COLOR

We have chosen the colors we like, and that feel suitable for the breed, mainly using Cascade Yarns with their wide color range. You can, of course, use any color; make sure the colors are not too close to each other otherwise your dog may "vanish". Contrast between dog and background is important.

POSITION OF THE DOG ON THE SWEATER

We have designed the sweaters mainly with the dogs in the center. This is a personal choice; you can move the dog up or down, or wrap the dog around the side of the sweater, knitting the head on the front and the tail end on the back of the sweater. The child's Dachshund pattern is a good example of an alternative position for the dog (see page 86).

KNITTING GRAPH PAPER

To create your own designs you will need knitting graph paper. There are plenty of sites online for sourcing knitting graph paper – we use the site www.theknittingsite.com. The "squares" are oblong and reflect the shape of stitches.

CUSTOMIZING THE CHARTS

All dogs have their own markings. You can alter the markings to match your dog using knitting graph paper. If your dog has a longer body, for example, add a couple of stitches; for shorter legs, take off a couple of rows. The Labradoodle could be a Cockapoo, for instance, by shortening the legs by a couple of rows and taking a couple of stitches out of the length of the body.

POSITION OF LETTERING ON THE SWEATER

When making a lettering sweater, use graph paper and copy the letters from the alphabet, leaving one or two stitches between each letter. For dog names, a space of ¾–1¼in/2–3cm between the top of the letters and the start of the dog will make the name stand out but still feel part of the image.

BACKGROUND SHAPES

Some of the dogs are knitted on a square or oval in a contrasting color. For the square, work 4 rows of color before you start the dog and 4 rows after finishing the dog. Add about 3 stitches to either side of the dog in the contrast square color. For the oval, using the Pug chart as an example (see page 126), copy the dog onto graph paper and draw an oval around the dog, leaving a few rows/stitches between the dog and the edge of the oval. Again, color choice is important: make sure you have a strong contrast between the colors otherwise your dog may not stand out.

ADULT SWEATERS

We have three basic patterns: two for women and one for men.
The Woman's Raglan Pullover is neat and boxy. The Woman's Long
and Loose Pullover is exactly as described: easy to wear and suitable
for most body shapes. The Man's Pullover is a relaxed style with set-
in sleeves. All the adult sweaters are in worsted-weight yarn in simple
stockinette stitch, so they are relatively quick to knit. The dogs are all
knitted in intarsia, so it helps to have some experience of color knitting.
Once you have decided on the shape, choose your breed; all of the
breeds are pictured on pages 22–27 to help you make your selection.
Some breeds are more complicated than others. One-color dogs – the
Labrador, Lurcher, West Highland Terrier and Labradoodle – are the
easiest to knit, but none of the dogs are particularly difficult.

WOMAN'S RAGLAN PULLOVER

FINISHED MEASUREMENTS

Small
Chest: 19¼in/49cm
Length: 22in/56cm

Medium
Chest: 20in/51cm
Length: 23¼in/59cm

Large
Chest: 21in/53cm
Length: 23¼in/59cm

NEEDLES AND YARN
- US 6/4mm and US 8/5mm knitting needles if using Cascade yarn
- US 5/3.75mm and US 7/4.5mm knitting needles if using Debbie Bliss yarn
- Main color (mc): Cascade 220 Solids and Heathers (CYCA #4) or Debbie Bliss Donegal Luxury Tweed Aran (CYCA #4) yarn

Size	Small	Medium	Large
Cascade	475g (16½oz)	500g (17½oz)	525g (18½oz)
Debbie Bliss	450g (16oz)	475g (16½oz)	500g (17½oz)

- 10g (¼oz) of Cascade or Debbie Bliss yarn in contrast color (optional)

GAUGE
18 sts and 24 rows to 4in/10cm measured over st st using US 8/5mm needles for Cascade yarn or US 7/4.5mm needles for Debbie Bliss yarn

DOG ON FRONT
All of the dogs are different shapes and colors. For yarn requirements and knitting instructions, refer to the index of dogs on page 140. This will direct you to the instructions and chart for your chosen breed.

BACK
With smaller needles and mc, cast on 90 [94, 98] sts.
Work 10 rows k2, p2 rib.
NOTE: For version with contrast edge, use contrast yarn to cast on and work first rib row, then change to mc to complete rib.
Change to larger needles.
Beg with a k row, continue in st st until back measures 13½ [14¼, 14¼] in/ 34 [36, 36] cm, ending on a p row.
SHAPE ARMHOLES:
Bind off 3 [4, 4] sts at beg of next 2 rows. *(84 [86, 90] sts)*
Dec 1 st at each end of next and every other row 26 [27, 27] times, ending on a p row. *(32 [32, 36] sts)*

Leave rem 32 [32, 36] sts on a holder for neck edge.

FRONT
Work as for back to armhole shaping, positioning and knitting the dog as instructed for your chosen dog breed (see index of dogs, page 140).
Continue in st st until front measures 13½ [14¼, 14¼] in/34 [36, 36] cm, ending on a p row.
SHAPE ARMHOLES:
Bind off 3 [4, 4] sts at beg of next 2 rows. *(84 [86, 90] sts)*
Dec 1 st at each end of next and every other row 18 [18, 19] times, ending on a p row. *(48 [50, 52] sts)*

SHAPE FRONT NECK:
With RS facing, k2tog, k15 [16, 17], turn, leaving rem sts on a holder.
Work each side separately:
Dec 1 st at beg of next row and at neck edge of every following row 5 [5, 7] times, and then at neck edge of every other row 3 times, and **at the same time** continue raglan shaping by dec 1 st at armhole edge of every other row.
With RS facing, slip center 14 sts onto a holder for neck edge, rejoin yarn and k to last 2 sts, k2tog.
Complete to match first side, reversing shaping.

SLEEVES (MAKE 2)

With smaller needles, cast on
38 [42, 44] sts and work rib as for back.
Change to larger needles.

Beg with a k row, continue in st st,
shaping sides by inc 1 st at each
end of next and every following
6th row 15 times. *(68 [72, 74] sts)*
Continue straight until sleeve
measures 19 [19, 19¾] in/
48 [48, 50] cm, ending on a p row.

SHAPE SLEEVE TOP:

Bind off 3 [4, 4] sts at beg of next
2 rows. *(62 [64, 66] sts)*
Dec 1 st at each end of next and
every other row 26 [27, 27] times.
(10 [10, 12] sts)
Leave rem 10 [10, 12] sts on a holder
for neck edge.

FINISHING

Block each piece and, using a
warm iron and cloth, press all parts
except ribbing. Sew in ends. Using
backstitch or mattress stitch, sew
up raglan seams but leave left back
raglan open.

NECK BAND:

With smaller needles and mc and RS
facing, pick up 10 [10, 12] sts across
top of left sleeve, 15 [15, 16] sts down
left front neck shaping, 14 sts across
center front, 15 [15, 16] sts up right
front neck shaping, 10 [10, 12] sts
across top of right sleeve and
32 [32, 36] sts across back neck.
(96 [96, 106] sts)
Work 6 rows k2, p2 rib.
Bind off loosely in rib.

Using backstitch or mattress stitch,
sew up remaining raglan seam and
neck edge. Sew up side and sleeve
seams. Press with a damp cloth.

WOMAN'S LONG AND LOOSE PULLOVER

FINISHED MEASUREMENTS

Small
Chest: 23in/58cm
Length: 26in/66cm

Medium
Chest: 24½in/62cm
Length: 26¾in/68cm

Large
Chest: 26in/66cm
Length: 27½in/70cm

NEEDLES AND YARN
- US 6/4mm and US 8/5mm knitting needles if using Cascade yarn
- US 5/3.75mm and US 7/4.5mm knitting needles if using Debbie Bliss yarn
- Main color (mc): Cascade 220 Solids and Heathers (CYCA #4) or Debbie Bliss Donegal Luxury Tweed Aran (CYCA #4) yarn

Size	Small	Medium	Large
Cascade	575g (20oz)	600g (21oz)	625g (22oz)
Debbie Bliss	525g (18½oz)	550g (19¼oz)	575g (20oz)

- 10g (¼oz) of Cascade or Debbie Bliss yarn in contrast color (optional)

GAUGE
18 sts and 24 rows to 4in/10cm measured over st st using US 8/5mm needles for Cascade yarn or US 7/4.5mm needles for Debbie Bliss yarn

DOG ON FRONT
All of the dogs are different shapes and colors. For yarn requirements and knitting instructions, refer to the index of dogs on page 140. This will direct you to the instructions and chart for your chosen breed.

BACK
With smaller needles and mc, cast on 106 [114, 122] sts.
Work 20 rows k2, p2 rib.
NOTE: For version with contrast edge, use contrast yarn to cast on and work first rib row, then change to mc to complete rib.
Change to larger needles.
Beg with a k row, continue in st st until back measures 17 [17¾, 18½] in/ 43 [45, 47] cm, ending on a p row.
SHAPE ARMHOLES:
Bind off 8 sts at beg of next 2 rows.
(90 [98, 106] sts)

Continue straight until armhole measures 8in/20cm, ending on a p row.
SHAPE SHOULDERS:
Next row (RS): Bind off 6 [7, 8] sts, k24 [27, 30] including st used to bind off, turn, leaving rem sts on a holder.
Work each side separately:
Next row (WS): Dec 1 st at neck edge, p to end.
Next row (RS): Bind off 7 [8, 9] sts, k to end.
Next row (WS): Dec 1 st at neck edge, p to end.
Next row (RS): Bind off 7 [8, 9] sts, k to end.

Next row (WS): Dec 1 st at neck edge, p to end.
Next row (RS): Bind off rem 7 [8, 9] sts. With RS facing, slip center 30 sts onto a holder for neck edge, rejoin yarn and k to end. Complete to match first side, reversing shaping.

FRONT
Work as for back to armhole shaping, positioning and knitting the dog as instructed for your chosen dog breed (see index of dogs, page 140).
SHAPE ARMHOLES:
Bind off 8 sts at beg of next 2 rows.
(90 [98, 106] sts)

Continue straight until armhole measures 18 rows less than back to shoulder, ending on a p row.

SHAPE FRONT NECK:

With RS facing, k38 [42, 46], turn, leaving rem sts on a holder.

Work each side separately:

Dec 1 st at neck edge of every row 6 times, and then at neck edge of every other row 5 times. *(27 [31, 35] sts)*

Work 1 row straight, so front matches back at shoulder, ending on a p row.

SHAPE SHOULDER:

Next row (RS): Bind off 6 [7, 8] sts, k to end.

Next row (WS): Purl.

Next row (RS): Bind off 7 [8, 9] sts, k to end.

Next row (WS): Purl.

Next row (RS): Bind off 7 [8, 9] sts, k to end.

Next row (WS): Purl.

Next row (RS): Bind off rem 7 [8, 9] sts.

With RS facing, slip center 14 sts onto a holder, rejoin yarn and k to end. Work 1 row, then complete to match first side, reversing shaping.

SLEEVES (MAKE 2)

With smaller needles, cast on 40 sts and work rib as for back.

Change to larger needles.

Beg with a k row, continue in st st, shaping sides by inc 1 st at each end of next and every following 4th row 10 times, and then every 6th row 8 times. *(76 sts)*

Continue straight until sleeve measures 18 [18½, 18½] in/ 46 [47, 47] cm.

Bind off rem sts.

FINISHING

Block each piece and, using a warm iron and cloth, press all parts except ribbing. Sew in ends. Using

backstitch or mattress stitch, sew right shoulder together.

NECK BAND:

With smaller needles and mc and RS facing, starting at left front shoulder pick up 24 sts down left front neck shaping, 14 sts across center front, 24 sts up right front neck shaping, 6 sts down right back shaping, 34 sts across back neck and 6 sts up left back shaping. *(104 sts)*

Work 6 rows k2, p2 rib.

Bind off loosely in rib.

Using backstitch or mattress stitch, sew left shoulder together and neck edge. Sew bound-off edge of sleeve around armhole, and sew up side and sleeve seams. Press with a damp cloth.

MAN'S PULLOVER

FINISHED MEASUREMENTS

Small
Chest: 22in/56cm
Length: 27½in/70cm

Medium
Chest: 23½in/60cm
Length: 28¼in/72cm

Large
Chest: 24¾in/63cm
Length: 28¼in/72cm

NEEDLES AND YARN
- US 6/4mm and US 8/5mm knitting needles if using Cascade yarn
- US 5/3.75mm and US 7/4.5mm knitting needles if using Debbie Bliss yarn
- Main color (mc): Cascade 220 Solids and Heathers (CYCA #4) or Debbie Bliss Donegal Luxury Tweed Aran (CYCA #4) yarn

Size	Small	Medium	Large
Cascade	575g (20oz)	600g (21oz)	625g (22oz)
Debbie Bliss	525g (18½oz)	550g (19¼oz)	575g (20oz)

- 10g (¼oz) of Cascade or Debbie Bliss yarn in contrast color (optional)

GAUGE
18 sts and 24 rows to 4in/10cm measured over st st using US 8/5mm needles for Cascade yarn or US 7/4.5mm needles for Debbie Bliss yarn

DOG ON FRONT
All of the dogs are different shapes and colors. For yarn requirements and knitting instructions, refer to the index of dogs on page 140. This will direct you to the instructions and chart for your chosen breed.

BACK
With smaller needles and mc, cast on 104 [110, 116] sts.
Work 16 rows k2, p2 rib.
NOTE: For version with contrast edge, use contrast yarn to cast on and work first rib row, then change to mc to complete rib.
Change to larger needles.
Beg with a k row, continue in st st until back measures 17 [17¾, 17¾] in/ 43 [45, 45] cm, ending on a p row.
SHAPE ARMHOLES:
Bind off 5 sts at beg of next 2 rows. *(94 [100, 106] sts)*
Dec 1 st at each end of next 5 rows, and then at each end of every other row 6 [7, 8] times. *(72 [76, 80] sts)*
Continue straight until armhole measures 9½in/24cm, ending on a p row.
SHAPE SHOULDERS:
Next row (RS): Bind off 5 [5, 6] sts, k17 [19, 20] including st used to bind off, turn, leaving rem sts on a holder.
Work each side separately:
Next row (WS): Dec 1 st at neck edge, p to end.
Next row (RS): Bind off 5 [5, 6] sts, k to end.
Next row (WS): Dec 1 st at neck edge, p to end.
Next row (RS): Bind off 5 [6, 6] sts, k to end.
Next row (WS): Purl.
Next row (RS): Bind off rem 5 [6, 6] sts.
With RS facing, slip center 28 sts onto a holder for neck edge, rejoin yarn and k to end. Complete to match first side, reversing shaping.

FRONT
Work as for back to armhole shaping, positioning and knitting the dog as instructed for your chosen dog breed (see index of dogs, page 140).
SHAPE ARMHOLES:
Work as for back, but continue in st st until armhole measures 6¾in/17cm, ending on a p row.
SHAPE FRONT NECK:
With RS facing, k29 [31, 33], turn, leaving rem sts on a holder.
Work each side separately:
Dec 1 st at neck edge of every row 6 times, and then at neck edge of every

other row 3 times. *(20 [22, 24] sts)*
Continue straight until front matches
back at shoulder, ending on a p row.
SHAPE SHOULDER:
Next row (RS): Bind off 5 [5, 6] sts,
k to end.
Next row (WS): Purl.
Next row (RS): Bind off 5 [5, 6] sts,
k to end.
Next row (WS): Purl.
Next row (RS): Bind off 5 [6, 6] sts,
k to end.
Next row (WS): Purl.
Next row (RS): Bind off rem
5 [6, 6] sts.
With RS facing, slip center 14 sts
onto a holder, rejoin yarn and k to
end. Complete to match first side,
reversing shaping.

SLEEVES (MAKE 2)
With smaller needles, cast on 44 sts
and work rib as for back.

Change to larger needles.
Beg with a k row, continue in st st,
shaping sides by inc 1 st at each end of
next and every following 8th [7th, 7th]
row 13 [14, 16] times. *(70 [72, 76] sts)*
Continue straight until sleeve
measures 20½ [20½, 21¼] in/
52 [52, 54] cm, ending
on a p row.
SHAPE SLEEVE TOP:
Bind off 5 sts at beg of next 2 rows.
(60 [62, 66] sts)
Dec 1 st at each end of next
5 [5, 6] rows. *(50 [52, 54] sts)*
Dec 1 st at each end of every other
row 13 times. *(24 [26, 28] sts)*
Dec 1 st at each end of every row
4 times. *(16 [18, 20] sts)*
Bind off rem sts.

FINISHING
Block each piece and, using a
warm iron and cloth, press all parts

except ribbing. Sew in ends. Using
backstitch or mattress stitch, sew right
shoulder together.
NECK BAND: With smaller needles
and mc and RS facing, starting at left
front shoulder pick up 20 sts down
left front neck shaping, 14 sts across
center front, 20 sts up right front
neck shaping, 6 sts down right back
shaping, 28 sts across back neck and
5 sts up left back shaping. *(92 sts)*
Work 8 rows k2, p2 rib. Bind off
loosely in rib.

Using backstitch or mattress stitch,
sew left shoulder together and
neck edge. Set in sleeves and sew up
side and sleeve seams. Press with a
damp cloth.

Labrador

PAGE 28

Easy

Lurcher

PAGE 30

Easy

Beagle

PAGE 32

Difficult

Dalmatian

PAGE 34

Easy

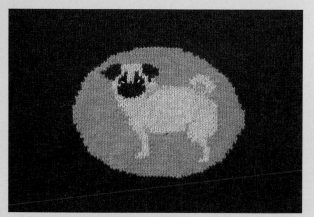

Pug

PAGE 36

Intermediate

Golden Retriever

PAGE 40

Intermediate

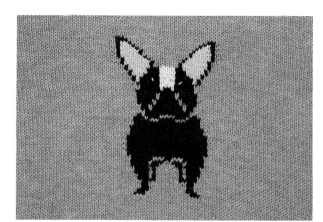

French Bulldog

PAGE 38

Intermediate

Chihuahua

PAGE 42

Easy

Staffordshire Bull Terrier

PAGE 46

Intermediate

Springer Spaniel

PAGE 44

Intermediate

Labradoodle

PAGE 48

Easy

Jack Russell

PAGE 50

Easy

Miniature Schnauzer

PAGE 52

Easy

Whippet

PAGE 54

Intermediate

Border Collie

PAGE 58

Easy

Border Terrier

PAGE 56

Intermediate

Dachshund

PAGE 62

Easy

West Highland Terrier

PAGE 60

Easy

Cave Canem
(Beware of the Dog)

PAGE 64

Easy

LABRADOR

YARN
- Main color: Debbie Bliss Donegal Luxury Tweed Aran (CYCA #4) in 54 Sky (mc); see pullover pattern for quantity
- 15g (½oz) of Cascade 220 Solids and Heathers (CYCA #4) in 8555 Black (bl)
- Tiny amount of worsted-weight yarn in brown (br) for eye

CHART
See page 125

WOMAN'S RAGLAN PULLOVER (PAGE 16)
Continue in st st until front measures 7½ [8, 8] in/19 [20, 20] cm, ending on a p row.
Follow chart for Labrador.
Row 1: K24 [26, 28] mc, k3bl, k28mc, k3bl, k32 [34, 36] mc.
Continue chart pattern until dog is finished.

WOMAN'S LONG AND LOOSE PULLOVER (PAGE 18)
Continue in st st until front measures 11½ [11¾, 12¼] in/29 [30, 31] cm, ending on a p row.
Follow chart for Labrador.
Row 1: K32 [36, 40] mc, k3bl, k28mc, k3bl, k40 [44, 48] mc.
Continue chart pattern until dog is finished.

MAN'S PULLOVER (PAGE 20)
Continue in st st until front measures 11½ [11½, 11¾] in/29 [29, 30] cm, ending on a p row.
Follow chart for Labrador.
Row 1: K31 [34, 37] mc, k3bl, k28mc, k3bl, k39 [42, 45] mc.
Continue chart pattern until dog is finished.

FINISHING DETAILS
Eye: With br, make a 3-loop French knot for eye.

LURCHER

YARN
- Main color: Cascade 220 Solids and Heathers (CYCA #4) in 9450 Smoke Heather (mc); see pullover pattern for quantity
- Contrast color: 50g (2oz) of Cascade 220 Solids and Heathers in 4002 Jet – charcoal (ch)
- 15g (½oz) of Rowan Kidsilk Haze (CYCA #2) in 00664 Steel and 00639 Anthracite (mohair – mo) – use FOUR strands together throughout (TWO strands of each color)

CHART
See page 125

WOMAN'S RAGLAN PULLOVER (PAGE 16)
This is an example for knitting the Lurcher without a square.
Continue in st st until front measures 8¼ [8¾, 8¾] in/21 [22, 22] cm, ending on a p row.
Follow chart for Lurcher.
Row 1: K46 [48, 50] mc, k2mo, k42 [44, 46] mc.
Continue chart pattern until dog is finished.

WOMAN'S LONG AND LOOSE PULLOVER (PAGE 18)
This is an example for knitting the Lurcher without a square.
Continue in st st until front measures 12½ [12½, 13] in/32 [32, 33] cm, ending on a p row.
Follow chart for Lurcher.
Row 1: K54 [58, 62] mc, k2mo, k50 [54, 58] mc.
Continue chart pattern until dog is finished.

MAN'S PULLOVER (PAGE 20)
Our Lurcher is knitted on a contrast square. Continue in st st until front measures 12¼ [12½, 13] in/ 31 [32, 33] cm, ending on a p row.
NOTE: For version without a contrast square, work all ch sts in mc.
Row 1: K30 [33, 36] mc, k44ch, k30 [33, 36] mc.
Work 5 rows st st, colors as set. Then follow chart for Lurcher.
Row 7: K30 [33, 36] mc, k23ch, k2mo, k19ch, k30 [33, 36] mc.
Continue chart pattern until dog is finished.
Work 7 rows to match bottom of square, ending on a k row.
Continue in mc.

BEAGLE

YARN
- Main color: Cascade 220 Solids and Heathers (CYCA #4) in 8555 Black (mc); see pullover pattern for quantity
- Contrast color: 50g (2oz) of Cascade 220 Solids and Heathers in 9451 Lake Chelan Heather – green (gn)
- 15g (½oz) of Cascade 220 Solids and Heathers in 8505 White (wh)
- 10g (¼oz) of Cascade 220 Solids and Heathers in 2415 Sunflower – gold (gd)
- 10g (¼oz) of Cascade 220 Solids and Heathers in 8555 Black (bl)

CHART
See page 120

WOMAN'S RAGLAN PULLOVER (PAGE 16)
Our Beagle is knitted on a contrast square. Continue in st st until front measures 8 [8¼, 8¼] in/ 20 [21, 21] cm, ending on a k row.
NOTE: For version without a contrast square, work all gn sts in mc.
Row 1: P17 [19, 21] mc, p56gn, p17 [19, 21] mc.
Work 2 rows st st, colors as set. Then follow chart for Beagle.
Row 4: K17 [19, 21] mc, k35gn, k3wh, k18gn, k17 [19, 21] mc.
Continue chart pattern until dog is finished.
Work 3 rows to match bottom of square, ending on a k row.
Continue in mc.

WOMAN'S LONG AND LOOSE PULLOVER (PAGE 18)
This is an example for knitting the Beagle without a square.
Continue in st st until front measures 12½ [13, 13½] in/32 [33, 34] cm, ending on a p row.
Follow chart for Beagle.
Row 1: K61 [65, 69] mc, k3wh, k42 [46, 50] mc.
Continue chart pattern until dog is finished.

MAN'S PULLOVER (PAGE 20)
This is an example for knitting the Beagle without a square.
Continue in st st until front measures 12½ [12½, 13] in/32 [32, 33] cm, ending on a p row.
Follow chart for Beagle.
Row 1: K60 [63, 66] mc, k3wh, k41 [44, 47] mc.
Continue chart pattern until dog is finished.

DALMATIAN

YARN
- Main color: Cascade 220 Solids and Heathers (CYCA #4) in 8836 Stonewash – blue lovat (mc); see pullover pattern for quantity
- 15g (½oz) of Cascade 220 Solids and Heathers in 8505 White (wh)
- 10g (¼oz) of Cascade 220 Solids and Heathers in 8555 Black (bl)

CHART
See page 122

WOMAN'S RAGLAN PULLOVER (PAGE 16)
Continue in st st until front measures 7½ [8, 8] in/19 [20, 20] cm, ending on a p row.
Follow chart for Dalmatian.
Row 1: K24 [26, 28] mc, k3wh, k28mc, k3wh, k32 [34, 36] mc.
Continue chart pattern until dog is finished.

WOMAN'S LONG AND LOOSE PULLOVER (PAGE 18)
Continue in st st until front measures 11½ [11¾, 12¼] in/29 [30, 31] cm, ending on a p row.
Follow chart for Dalmatian.
Row 1: K32 [36, 40] mc, k3wh, k28mc, k3wh, k40 [44, 48] mc.
Continue chart pattern until dog is finished.

MAN'S PULLOVER (PAGE 20)
Continue in st st until front measures 11½ [11½, 11¾] in/29 [29, 30] cm, ending on a p row.
Follow chart for Dalmatian.
Row 1: K31 [34, 37] mc, k3wh, k28mc, k3wh, k39 [42, 45] mc.
Continue chart pattern until dog is finished.

PUG

YARN

- Main color: Cascade 220 Solids and Heathers (CYCA #4) in 4002 Jet – charcoal (mc); see pullover pattern for quantity
- Contrast color: 50g (2oz) of Cascade 220 Solids and Heathers in 9325 Westpoint Blue Heather – sky blue (bu)
- 20g (¾oz) of Cascade 220 Solids and Heathers in 2442 Fog Hatt – oatmeal (oa)
- 5g (⅛oz) of Cascade 220 Solids and Heathers in 4002 Jet – charcoal (ch)
- Tiny amount of Cascade 220 Solids and Heathers in 8555 Black (bl) for eyes
- Tiny amount of Cascade 220 Solids and Heathers in 8505 White (wh) for eyes

CHART

See page 126

WOMAN'S RAGLAN PULLOVER (PAGE 16)

This is an example for knitting the Pug without an oval.

Continue in st st until front measures 9 [9½, 9½] in/23 [24, 24] cm, ending on a p row.

Follow chart pattern for Pug.

Row 1: K30 [32, 34] mc, k3oa, k16mc, k3oa, k38 [40, 42] mc.

Continue chart pattern until dog is finished.

WOMAN'S LONG AND LOOSE PULLOVER (PAGE 18)

Our Pug is knitted on a contrast oval.

Continue in st st until front measures 10¾ [11, 11½] in/27 [28, 29] cm, ending on a k row.

NOTE: For version without a contrast oval, work all bu sts in mc.

Follow chart for Pug in oval.

Row 1: P46 [50, 54] mc, p14bu, p46 [50, 54] mc.

Continue to follow chart for oval.

START OF PUG:

Row 8: K35 [39, 43] mc, k3bu, k3oa, k16bu, k3oa, k11bu, k35 [39, 43] mc.

Continue chart pattern until dog is finished, then follow chart for last 7 rows of oval, ending on a k row. Continue in mc.

MAN'S PULLOVER (PAGE 20)

This is an example for knitting the Pug without an oval.

Continue in st st until front measures 11¾ [11¾, 12¼] in/30 [30, 31] cm, ending on a p row.

Follow chart for Pug.

Row 1: K37 [40, 43] mc, k3oa, k16mc, k3oa, k45 [48, 51] mc.

Continue chart pattern until dog is finished.

FINISHING DETAILS

Eyes: With bl, make a 3-loop French knot for each eye and sew a small slanting stitch on top in wh.

FRENCH BULLDOG

YARN

- Main color: Cascade 220 Solids and Heathers (CYCA #4) in 2442 Fog Hatt – oatmeal (mc); see pullover pattern for quantity
- 15g (½oz) of Cascade 220 Solids and Heather in 4002 Jet – charcoal (ch)
- 5g (⅛oz) of Cascade 220 Solids and Heather in 8505 White (wh)
- 5g (⅛oz) of Cascade 220 Solids and Heather in 4192 Soft Pink (pk)
- Tiny amount of Cascade 220 Solids and Heather in 8555 Black (bl) for eyes

CHART
See page 123

WOMAN'S RAGLAN PULLOVER (PAGE 16)
Continue in st st until front measures 8 [8¼, 8¼] in/20 [21, 21] cm, ending on a p row.
Follow chart for French Bulldog.
Row 1: K36 [38, 40] mc, k3ch, k12mc, k3ch, k36 [38, 40] mc.
Continue chart pattern until dog is finished.

WOMAN'S LONG AND LOOSE PULLOVER (PAGE 18)
Continue in st st until front measures 11¾ [12¼, 12½] in/30 [31, 32] cm, ending on a p row.
Follow chart for French Bulldog.
Row 1: K44 [48, 52] mc, k3ch, k12mc, k3ch, k44 [48, 52] mc.
Continue chart pattern until dog is finished.

MAN'S PULLOVER (PAGE 20)
Continue in st st until front measures 12¼ [12¼, 12½] in/31 [31, 32] cm, ending on a p row.
Follow chart for French Bulldog.
Row 1: K43 [46, 49] mc, k3ch, k12mc, k3ch, k43 [46, 49] mc.
Continue chart pattern until dog is finished.

FINISHING DETAILS
Eyes: With bl, make a 3-loop French knot for each eye and sew a small slanting stitch on top in wh.

GOLDEN RETRIEVER

YARN AND NEEDLES

- Main color: Cascade 220 Solids and Heathers (CYCA #4) in 9325 in Westpoint Blue Heather – sky blue (mc); see pullover pattern for quantity
- 15g (½oz) of Cascade 220 Solids and Heathers in 9499 Sand – fawn (fn)
- Small amount of Cascade 220 Solids and Heathers in 4002 Jet – charcoal (ch) for lettering
- Tiny amount of Cascade 220 Solids and Heathers in 8555 Black (bl) for eye and nose
- Small amount of worsted-weight yarn for collar (optional)
- US 6/4mm knitting needles for collar (optional)

CHARTS

See page 123 for dog
See page 130 for lettering

WOMAN'S RAGLAN PULLOVER (PAGE 16)

NOTE: There is no room for lettering on the raglan pullover.

Continue in st st until front measures 8 [8¼, 8¼] in/20 [21, 21] cm, ending on a p row.

Follow chart for Golden Retriever.

Row 1: K29 [31, 33] mc, k3fn, k27mc, k3fn, k28 [30, 32] mc.

Continue chart pattern until dog is finished.

WOMAN'S LONG AND LOOSE PULLOVER (PAGE 18)

Continue in st st until front measures 8 [8¼, 8¾] in/20 [21, 22] cm, ending on a p row.

Follow chart for lettering; Hugo is an example.

Row 1: K34 [38, 42] mc, k3ch, k9mc, k4ch, k8mc, k3ch, k5mc, k2ch, k6mc k2ch, k30 [34, 38] mc.

Continue chart pattern until lettering is finished, ending on a p row.

Work 6 rows st st, ending on a p row.

Follow chart for Golden Retriever.

Next row: K37 [41, 45] mc, k3fn, k27mc, k3fn, k36 [40, 44] mc.

Continue chart pattern until dog is finished.

MAN'S PULLOVER (PAGE 20)

Continue in st st until front measures 8 [8, 8¼] in/20 [20, 21] cm, ending on a p row.

Follow chart for lettering; Hugo is an example.

Row 1: K33 [36, 39] mc, k3ch, k9mc, k4ch, k8mc, k3ch, k5mc, k2ch, k6mc, k2ch, k29 [32, 35] mc.

Continue chart pattern until lettering is finished, ending on a p row.

Work 6 rows st st, ending on a p row.

Follow chart for Golden Retriever.

Next row: K36 [39, 42] mc, k3fn, k27mc, k3fn, k35 [38, 41] mc.

Continue chart pattern until dog is finished.

FINISHING DETAILS

Eye: With bl, make a 3-loop French knot for eye.

Collar: With US 6/4mm needles and collar color, cast on 28 sts and knit 2 rows. Bind off. Push each end into the side of the dog's neck, and sew collar ends together on reverse side of pullover (optional, see page 23).

CHIHUAHUA

YARN
- Main color: Debbie Bliss Donegal Luxury Tweed Aran (CYCA #4) in 15 Charcoal (mc); see pullover pattern for quantity
- 15g (½oz) of Cascade 220 Solids and Heathers (CYCA #4) in 9499 Sand – fawn (fn)
- 5g (⅛oz) of Cascade 220 Solids and Heathers in 4192 Soft Pink (pk)
- Tiny amount of Cascade 220 Solids and Heathers in 8555 Black (bl) for eyes and nose

CHART
See page 121

WOMAN'S RAGLAN PULLOVER (PAGE 16)
Continue in st st until front measures 8¼ [8¾, 8¾] in/21 [22, 22] cm, ending on a p row.
Follow chart for Chihuahua.
Row 1: K29 [31, 33] mc, k2fn, k18mc, k2fn, k39 [41, 43] mc.
Continue chart pattern until dog is finished.

WOMAN'S LONG AND LOOSE PULLOVER (PAGE 18)
Continue in st st until front measures 12½ [13, 13½] in/32 [33, 34] cm, ending on a p row.
Follow chart for Chihuahua.
Row 1: K37 [41, 45] mc, k2fn, k18mc, k2fn, k47 [51, 55] mc.
Continue chart pattern until dog is finished.

MAN'S PULLOVER (PAGE 20)
Continue in st st until front measures 12½ [12½, 13] in/32 [32, 33] cm, ending on a p row.
Follow chart for Chihuahua.
Row 1: K36 [39, 42] mc, k2fn, k18mc, k2fn, k46 [49, 52] mc.
Continue chart pattern until dog is finished.

FINISHING DETAILS
Eyes: With bl, make a 4-loop French knot for each eye.

SPRINGER SPANIEL

YARN

- Main color: Cascade 220 Solids and Heathers (CYCA #4) in 9635 Mineral Blue (mc); see pullover pattern for quantity
- 15g (½oz) of Cascade 220 Solids and Heathers in 2403 Chocolate – mahogany (ma)
- 10g (¼oz) of Cascade 220 Solids and Heathers in 8505 White (wh)
- Tiny amount of Cascade 220 Solids and Heathers in 8555 Black (bl) for eye and nose

CHART

See page 127

WOMAN'S RAGLAN PULLOVER (PAGE 16)

Continue in st st until front measures 8¼ [8¾, 8¾] in/21 [22, 22] cm, ending on a p row.

Follow chart for Springer Spaniel.

Row 1: K29 [31, 33] mc, k3ma, k26mc, k3wh, k29 [31, 33] mc.

Continue chart pattern until dog is finished.

WOMAN'S LONG AND LOOSE PULLOVER (PAGE 18)

Continue in st st until front measures 12½ [13, 13½] in/32 [33, 34] cm, ending on a p row.

Follow chart for Springer Spaniel.

Row 1: K37 [41, 45] mc, k3ma, k26mc, k3wh, k37 [41, 45] mc.

Continue chart pattern until dog is finished.

MAN'S PULLOVER (PAGE 20)

Continue in st st until front measures 12½ [12½, 13] in/32 [32, 33] cm, ending on a p row.

Follow chart for Springer Spaniel.

Row 1: K36 [39, 42] mc, k3ma, k26mc, k3wh, k36 [39, 42] mc.

Continue chart pattern until dog is finished.

FINISHING DETAILS

Eye: With bl, make a 3-loop French knot for eye.

STAFFORDSHIRE BULL TERRIER

YARN

- Main color: Debbie Bliss Donegal Luxury Tweed Aran (CYCA #4) in 52 Lavender (mc); see pullover pattern for quantity
- Contrast color: 10g (¼oz) of Cascade 220 Solids and Heathers (CYCA #4) in 2442 Fog Hatt – oatmeal (oa)
- 20g (¾oz) of Cascade 220 Solids and Heathers in 2442 Fog Hatt – oatmeal (oa)
- 15g (½oz) of Cascade 220 Solids and Heathers in 9465 Burnt Orange – brown (br)
- 5g (⅛oz) of Cascade 220 Solids and Heathers in 8505 White (wh)
- Tiny amount of Cascade 220 Solids and Heathers in 8555 Black (bl) for eye and nose

CHART

See page 127

WOMAN'S RAGLAN PULLOVER (PAGE 16)

This is an example for knitting the Staffordshire Bull Terrier without a square.
Continue in st st until front measures 8 [8¼, 8¼] in/20 [21, 21] cm, ending on a p row.
Follow chart for Staffordshire Bull Terrier.
Row 1: K38 [40, 42] mc, k3br, k49 [51, 53] mc.
Continue chart pattern until dog is finished.

WOMAN'S LONG AND LOOSE PULLOVER (PAGE 18)

This is an example for knitting the Staffordshire Bull Terrier without a square.
Continue in st st until front measures 11¾ [12¼, 12½] in/30 [31, 32] cm, ending on a p row.
Follow chart for Staffordshire Bull Terrier.
Row 1: K46 [50, 54] mc, k3br, k57 [61, 65] mc.
Continue chart pattern until dog is finished.

MAN'S PULLOVER (PAGE 20)

Our Staffordshire Bull Terrier is knitted on a contrast square.
Continue in st st until front measures 11¾ [12¼, 12¼] in/29.5 [31, 31] cm, ending on a p row.
NOTE: For version without a contrast square, work all oa sts in mc.
Row 1: K23 [26, 29] mc, k58oa, k23 [26, 29] mc.
Work 3 rows st st, colors as set.
Follow chart for Staffordshire Bull Terrier.
Row 5: K23 [26, 29] mc, k22oa, k3br, k33oa, k23 [26, 29] mc.
Continue chart pattern until dog is finished.
Work 4 rows to match bottom of square, ending on a k row.
Continue in mc.

FINISHING DETAILS

Eye: With bl, make a 3-loop French knot for eye.

LABRADOODLE

YARN

- Main color: Cascade 220 Solids and Heathers (CYCA #4) in 8393 Navy (mc); see pullover pattern for quantity
- Contrast edge: 10g (¼oz) of Cascade 220 Solids and Heathers in 8010 Natural – cream (cr)
- 15g (½oz) of Drops Alpaca Bouclé (CYCA #4) in 0100 Off White (ow)
- Tiny amount of Cascade 220 Solids and Heathers in 8555 Black (bl) for eyes and nose

CHART

See page 124

WOMAN'S RAGLAN PULLOVER (PAGE 16)

Continue in st st until front measures 8 [8¼, 8¼] in/20 [21, 21] cm, ending on a p row.
Follow chart for Labradoodle.
Row 1: K50 [52, 54] mc, k3ow, k37 [39, 41] mc.
Continue chart pattern until dog is finished.

WOMAN'S LONG AND LOOSE PULLOVER (PAGE 18)

Continue in st st until front measures 11¾ [12¼, 12½] in/30 [31, 32] cm, ending on a p row.
Follow chart for Labradoodle.
Row 1: K58 [62, 66] mc, k3ow, k45 [49, 53] mc.
Continue chart pattern until dog is finished.

MAN'S PULLOVER (PAGE 20)

Continue in st st until front measures 12¼ [12¼, 12½] in/31 [31, 32] cm, ending on a p row.
Follow chart for Labradoodle.
Row 1: K57 [60, 63] mc, k3ow, k44 [47, 50] mc.
Continue chart pattern until dog is finished.

FINISHING DETAILS

Eyes: With bl, make 1 duplicate stitch for each eye.

JACK RUSSELL

YARN
- Main color: Cascade 220 Solids and Heathers (CYCA #4) in 8010 Natural – cream (mc); see pullover pattern for quantity
- Contrast color: 50g (2oz) of Cascade 220 Solids and Heathers in 8400 Charcoal Grey (gr)
- 15g (½oz) of Cascade 220 Solids and Heathers in 8010 Natural – cream (cr)
- 10g (¼oz) of Cascade 220 Solids and Heathers in 8013 Walnut Heather – fawn (fn)
- Tiny amount of Cascade 220 Solids and Heathers in 8555 Black (bl) for eyes and nose

CHART
See page 124

WOMAN'S RAGLAN PULLOVER (PAGE 16)
Our Jack Russell is knitted on a contrast square. Continue in st st until front measures 8¼ [8¾, 8¾] in/ 21 [22, 22] cm, ending on a p row.
NOTE: For version without a contrast square, work all gr sts in mc.
Row 1: K21 [23, 25] mc, k48gr, k21 [23, 25] mc.
Work 5 rows st st, colors as set.
Then follow chart for Jack Russell.
Row 7: K21 [23, 25] mc, k11gr, k2cr, k17gr, k2cr, k16gr, k21 [23, 25] mc.
Continue chart pattern until dog is finished.
Work 6 rows to match bottom of square, ending on a k row.
Continue in mc.

WOMAN'S LONG AND LOOSE PULLOVER (PAGE 18)
This is an example for knitting the Jack Russell without a square.
Continue in st st until front measures 13 [13½, 13¾] in/33 [34, 35] cm, ending on a p row.
Follow chart for Jack Russell.
Row 1: K40 [44, 48] mc, k2cr, k17mc, k2cr, k45 [49, 53] mc.
Continue chart pattern until dog is finished.

MAN'S PULLOVER (PAGE 20)
This is an example for knitting the Jack Russell without a square.
Continue in st st until front measures 13½ [13¾, 13¾] in/34 [35, 35] cm, ending on a p row.
Follow chart for Jack Russell.
Row 1: K39 [42, 45] mc, k2cr, k17mc, k2cr, k44 [47, 50] mc.
Continue chart pattern until dog is finished.

FINISHING DETAILS
Eye: With bl, make a 3-loop French knot for eye.

MINIATURE SCHNAUZER

YARN AND MATERIALS
- Main color: Debbie Bliss Donegal Luxury Tweed Aran (CYCA #4) in 53 Meadow (mc); see pullover pattern for quantity
- 15g (½oz) of Rowan Kidsilk Haze (CYCA #2) in 00634 Cream (mohair – mo) – use FOUR strands together throughout
- 15g (½oz) of Cascade 220 Solids and Heathers (CYCA #4) in 8400 Charcoal Grey (gr)
- 5g (⅛oz) of Cascade 220 Solids and Heathers in 8555 Black (bl)
- 2 black beads for eyes, plus sewing needle and black thread for sewing on

CHART
See page 126

WOMAN'S RAGLAN PULLOVER (PAGE 16)
Continue in st st until front measures 7½ [8, 8] in/19 [20, 20] cm, ending on a p row.
Follow chart for Miniature Schnauzer.
Row 1: K46 [48, 50] mc, k5mo, k39 [41, 43] mc.
Continue chart pattern, working loopy st with mo for eyebrows, until dog is finished.

WOMAN'S LONG AND LOOSE PULLOVER (PAGE 18)
Continue in st st until front measures 11½ [11¾, 12¼] in/29 [30, 31] cm, ending on a p row.
Follow chart for Miniature Schnauzer.
Row 1: K54 [58, 62] mc, k5mo, k47 [51, 55] mc.
Continue chart pattern, working loopy st with mo for eyebrows, until dog is finished.

MAN'S PULLOVER (PAGE 20)
Continue in st st until front measures 11½ [11½, 11¾] in/29 [29, 30] cm, ending on a p row.
Follow chart for Miniature Schnauzer.
Row 1: K53 [56, 59] mc, k5mo, k46 [49, 52] mc.
Continue chart pattern, working loopy st with mo for eyebrows, until dog is finished.

FINISHING DETAILS
Eyes: Sew on bead for each eye.

LOOPY STITCH
On a knit row, knit one stitch as normal but leave the stitch on the left-hand needle. Bring the yarn from the back to the front between the two needles. Loop the yarn around the index finger of your left hand. Take the yarn between the two needles to the back of the work. Knit the stitch from the left-hand needle as normal. You now have two stitches on the right-hand needle and a loop between them. Pass the first stitch over the second stitch to trap the loop, which is now secure. On a purl row, take the loop to the RS of the knitting and work knit stitches in purl.

WHIPPET

YARN
- Main color: Debbie Bliss Donegal Luxury Tweed Aran (CYCA #4) in 49 Rose (mc); see pullover pattern for quantity
- Contrast color: 60g (2¼oz) of Cascade 220 Solids and Heathers (CYCA #4) in 8400 Charcoal Grey (gr)
- 15g (½oz) of Cascade 220 Solids and Heathers in 8505 White (wh)
- 10g (¼oz) of Cascade 220 Solids and Heathers in 9499 Sand – fawn (fn)
- Tiny amount of Cascade 220 Solids and Heathers in 8555 Black (bl) for eye and nose

CHART
See page 128

WOMAN'S RAGLAN PULLOVER (PAGE 16)
Our Whippet is knitted on a contrast square. Continue in st st until front measures 8 [8¼, 8¼] in/ 20 [21, 21] cm, ending on a p row.
NOTE: For version without a contrast square, work all gr sts in mc.
Row 1: K13 [15, 17] mc, k64gr, k13 [15, 17] mc.
Work 3 rows st st, colors as set. Then follow chart for Whippet.
Row 5: K13 [15, 17] mc, k14gr, k2wh, k1gr, k1wh, k20gr, k1wh, k1gr, k2wh, k22gr, k13 [15, 17] mc.
Continue chart pattern until dog is finished.
Work 4 rows to match bottom of square, ending on a p row.
Continue in main color.

WOMAN'S LONG AND LOOSE PULLOVER (PAGE 18)
This is an example for knitting the Whippet without a square.
Continue in st st until front measures 12½, [12½, 13½] in/32 [32, 34] cm, ending on a p row.
Follow chart for Whippet.
Row 1: K35 [39, 43] mc, k2wh, k1mc, k1wh, k20mc, k1wh, k1mc, k2wh, k43 [47, 51] mc.
Continue chart pattern until dog is finished.

MAN'S PULLOVER (PAGE 20)
This is an example for knitting the Whippet without a square.
Continue in st st until front measures 12½, [12½, 13] in/32 [32, 33] cm, ending on a p row.
Follow chart for Whippet.
Row 1: K34 [37, 40] mc, k2wh, k1mc, k1wh, k20mc, k1wh, k1mc, k2wh, k42 [45, 48] mc.
Continue chart pattern until dog is finished.

FINISHING DETAILS
Eye: With bl, make a 3-loop French knot for eye.

BORDER TERRIER

YARN
- Main color: Cascade 220 Solids and Heathers (CYCA #4) in 8836 Stonewash – blue lovat (mc); see pullover pattern for quantity
- Contrast color: 50g (2oz) of Cascade 220 Solids and Heathers in 9600 Antiqued Heather – buttermilk (bt)
- 15g (½oz) of Cascade 220 Solids and Heathers in 2440 Vinci – coffee (co)
- 10g (¼oz) of Cascade 220 Solids and Heathers in 4002 Jet – charcoal (ch)

CHART
See page 121

WOMAN'S RAGLAN PULLOVER (PAGE 16)
This is an example for knitting the Border Terrier without a square. Continue in st st until front measures 8¼ [8¾, 8¾] in/21 [22, 22] cm, ending on a p row.
Follow chart for Border Terrier.
Row 1: K27 [29, 31] mc, k3co, k1mc, k2co, k19mc, k3co, k35 [37, 39] mc.
Continue chart pattern until dog is finished.

WOMAN'S LONG AND LOOSE PULLOVER (PAGE 18)
Our Border Terrier is knitted on a contrast square. Continue in st st until front measures 12¼ [12½, 13] in/ 31 [32, 33] cm, ending on a p row.
NOTE: For version without a contrast square, work all bt sts in mc.
Row 1: K22 [26, 30] mc, k62bt, k22 [26, 30] mc.
Work 3 rows st st, colors as set.
Then follow chart for Border Terrier.
Row 5: K22 [26, 30] mc, k13bt, k3co, k1bt, k2co, k19bt, k3co, k21bt, k22 [26, 30] mc.
Continue chart pattern until dog is finished.
Work 4 rows to match bottom of square, ending on a p row.
Continue in mc.

MAN'S PULLOVER (PAGE 20)
This is an example for knitting the Border Terrier without a square. Continue in st st until front measures 12½ [12½, 13] in/32 [32, 33] cm, ending on a p row.
Follow chart for Border Terrier.
Row 1: K34 [37, 40] mc, k3co, k1mc, k2co, k19mc, k3co, k42 [45, 48] mc.
Continue chart pattern until dog is finished.

BORDER COLLIE

YARN AND MATERIALS
- Main color: Cascade 220 Solids and Heathers (CYCA #4) in 9560 Liberty Heather – purple heather (mc); see pullover pattern for quantity
- Contrast edge: 10g (¼oz) of Cascade 220 Solids and Heathers in 9450 Smoke Heather – green heather (gh)
- 15g (½oz) of Cascade 220 Solids and Heathers in 8555 Black (bl)
- 15g (½oz) of Cascade 220 Solids and Heathers in 8505 White (wh)
- Black bead for eye, plus sewing needle and black thread for sewing on (optional)

CHART
See page 120

WOMAN'S RAGLAN PULLOVER (PAGE 16)
Continue in st st until front measures 8 [8¼, 8¼] in/20 [21, 21] cm, ending on a p row.
Follow chart for Border Collie.
Row 1: K34 [36, 38] mc, k2bl, k22mc, k3wh, k29 [31, 33] mc.
Continue chart pattern until dog is finished.

WOMAN'S LONG AND LOOSE PULLOVER (PAGE 18)
Continue in st st until front measures 10¾ [11, 11½] in/27 [28, 29] cm, ending on a p row.
Follow chart for Border Collie.
Row 1: K37 [41, 45] mc, k2bl, k22mc, k3wh, k42 [46, 50] mc.
Continue chart pattern until dog is finished.

MAN'S PULLOVER (PAGE 20)
Continue in st st until front measures 12¼ [12¼, 12½] in/31 [31, 32] cm, ending on a p row.
Follow chart for Border Collie.
Row 1: K36 [39, 42] mc, k2bl, k22mc, k3wh, k41 [44, 47] mc.
Continue chart pattern until dog is finished.

FINISHING DETAILS
Eye: Sew on black bead for eye.

WEST HIGHLAND TERRIER

YARN AND NEEDLES

- Main color: Cascade 220 Solids and Heathers (CYCA #4) in 9567 Smoky Blue – sage (mc); see pullover pattern for quantity
- 20g (¾oz) of Rowan Kidsilk Haze (CYCA #2) in 00634 Cream (mohair – mo) – use FOUR strands together throughout
- Tiny amount of Cascade 220 Solids and Heathers in 4192 Soft Pink (pk) for ears
- Tiny amount of Cascade 220 Solids and Heathers in 8555 Black (bl) for eye and nose
- Small amount of worsted-weight yarn for collar
- US 6/4mm knitting needles for collar

CHART

See page 128

WOMAN'S RAGLAN PULLOVER (PAGE 16)

Continue in st st until front measures 9 [9½, 9½] in/23 [24, 24] cm, ending on a p row.
Follow chart for West Highland Terrier.
Row 1: K28 [30, 32] mc, k3mo, k1mc, k1mo, k16mc, k1mo, k1mc, k3mo, k36 [38, 40] mc.
Continue chart pattern until dog is finished.

WOMAN'S LONG AND LOOSE PULLOVER (PAGE 18)

Continue in st st until front measures 13 [13½, 13¾] in/33 [34, 35] cm, ending on a p row.
Follow chart for West Highland Terrier.
Row 1: K36 [40, 44] mc, k3mo, k1mc, k1mo, k16mc, k1mo, k1mc, k3mo, k44 [48, 52] mc.
Continue chart pattern until dog is finished.

MAN'S PULLOVER (PAGE 20)

Continue in st st until front measures 13 [13, 13½] in/33 [33, 34] cm, ending on a p row.
Follow chart for West Highland Terrier.
Row 1: K35 [38, 41] mc, k3mo, k1mc, k1mo, k16mc, k1mo, k1mc, k3mo, k43 [46, 49] mc.
Continue chart pattern until dog is finished.

FINISHING DETAILS

Eye: With bl, make a 3-loop French knot for eye.
Collar: With US 6/4mm needles and collar color, cast on 28 sts and knit 2 rows. Bind off. Push each end into the side of the dog's neck, and sew collar ends together on reverse side of pullover.

DACHSHUND

YARN
- Main color: Cascade 220 Solids and Heathers (CYCA #4) in 8401 Silver Grey (mc); see pullover pattern for quantity
- 15g (½oz) of Cascade 220 Solids and Heathers in 8555 Black (bl)
- 5g (⅛oz) of Cascade 220 Solids and Heathers in 2415 Sunflower – gold (gd)

CHART
See page 122

WOMAN'S RAGLAN PULLOVER (PAGE 16)
Continue in st st until front measures 10¼ [10¾, 10¾] in/26 [27, 27] cm, ending on a p row.
Follow chart for Dachshund.
Row 1: K26 [28, 30] mc, k3gd, k27mc, k3gd, k31 [33, 35] mc.
Continue chart pattern until dog is finished.

WOMAN'S LONG AND LOOSE PULLOVER (PAGE 18)
Continue in st st until front measures 14½ [15¼, 16] in/37 [39, 41] cm, ending on a p row.
Follow chart for Dachshund.
Row 1: K34 [38, 42] mc, k3gd, k27mc, k3gd, k39 [43, 47] mc.
Continue chart pattern until dog is finished.

MAN'S PULLOVER (PAGE 20)
Continue in st st until front measures 14½ [14½, 15¼] in/37 [37, 39] cm, ending on a p row.
Follow chart for Dachshund.
Row 1: K33 [36, 39] mc, k3gd, k27mc, k3gd, k38 [41, 44] mc.
Continue chart pattern until dog is finished.

CAVE CANEM
(BEWARE OF THE DOG)

YARN
- Main color: Cascade 220 Solids and Heathers (CYCA #4) in 8555 Black (mc); see pullover pattern for quantity
- Contrast color: 15g (½oz) of Cascade 220 Solids and Heathers in 8505 White (wh)

NOTE: Use separate balls of contrast yarn for each letter. Take the main color across the back of each letter, weaving in when necessary (generally when carried over more than 3 stitches). Be careful not to pull the main color too tight or the knitting will pucker.

CHART
See page 129

WOMAN'S RAGLAN PULLOVER (PAGE 16)
Continue in st st until front measures 10 [10¼, 10¼] in/25 [26, 26] cm, ending on a p row.
Follow chart pattern for lettering.
Row 1: K16 [18, 20] mc, k2wh, k9mc, k2wh, k1mc, k9wh, k1mc, k2wh, k6mc, k2wh, k1mc, k2wh, k9mc, k2wh, k3mc, k3wh, k20 [22, 24] mc.
Continue chart pattern until lettering is finished.

WOMAN'S LONG AND LOOSE PULLOVER (PAGE 18)
Continue in st st until front measures 13½ [13¾, 14¼] in/34 [35, 36] cm, ending on a p row.
Follow chart for lettering.
Row 1: K24 [28, 32] mc, k2wh, k9mc, k2wh, k1mc, k9wh, k1mc, k2wh, k6mc, k2wh, k1mc, k2wh, k9mc, k2wh, k3mc, k3wh, k28 [32, 36] mc.
Continue chart pattern until lettering is finished.

MAN'S PULLOVER (PAGE 20)
Continue in st st until front measures 13½ [13½, 13¾] in/34 [34, 35] cm, ending on a p row.
Follow chart for lettering.
Row 1: K23 [26, 29] mc, k2wh, k9mc, k2wh, k1mc, k9wh, k1mc, k2wh, k6mc, k2wh, k1mc, k2wh, k9mc, k2wh, k3mc, k3wh, k27 [30, 33] mc.
Continue chart pattern until lettering is finished.

CHILD AND BABY
PULLOVERS AND CARDIGANS

We have one Child's Pullover shape, which is round-neck, with dropped shoulders, loose-fitting, and sized for ages 3–5, 5–7 and 7–9 years. The Baby's Raglan Pullover is in a round-neck, raglan, sweatshirt shape and is sized for ages 6–12 months, 1–2 years and 2–3 years. The Baby's Cardigan is round-neck, with set-in sleeves and pockets, and is sized for ages 0–3 months and 3–6 months. We have scaled down a selection of the adult-size dog charts for the child and baby sweaters. There are eight different dogs; all eight breeds are pictured on pages 76–79 to help you make your selection. The simplest are the Labrador and West Highland Terrier. For a quick knit, we recommend the Baby's Raglan Pullover: the perfect present for a dog-loving new parent.

CHILD'S PULLOVER

FINISHED MEASUREMENTS

Small
To fit age: 3–5 years
Chest: 13½in/34cm
Length: 15in/38cm

Medium
To fit age: 5–7 years
Chest: 14¼in/36cm
Length: 17in/43cm

Large
To fit age: 7–9 years
Chest: 15¼in/39cm
Length: 19¼in/49cm

NEEDLES AND YARN
- US 3/3.25mm knitting needles
- US 6/4mm knitting needles
- Main color (mc): Erika Knight British Blue Wool or Erika Knight British Blue 100 (CYCA #3)

Size	Small	Medium	Large
Quantity	200g (7oz)	230g (8oz)	280g (10oz)

- 10g (¼oz) of Erika Knight yarn in contrast color (optional)

GAUGE
22 sts and 30 rows to 4in/10cm measured over st st using US 6/4mm needles

DOG ON FRONT
All of the dogs are different shapes and colors. For yarn requirements and knitting instructions, refer to the index of dogs on page 140. This will direct you to the instructions and chart for your chosen breed.

BACK
With US 3/3.25mm needles and mc, cast on 76 [82, 88] sts.
Work 10 rows k1, p1 rib.
NOTE: For version with contrast edge, use contrast yarn to cast on and work first rib row, then change to mc to complete rib.
Change to US 6/4mm needles.
Beg with a k row, continue in st st until back measures 9 [11, 13] in/ 23 [28, 33] cm, ending on a p row.
SHAPE ARMHOLES:
Bind off 6 [7, 8] sts at beg of next 2 rows. (64 [68, 72] sts)
Continue straight until armhole measures 5½ [5½, 6] in/14 [14, 15] cm, ending on a p row.

SHAPE SHOULDERS:
Next row (RS): Bind off 6 [6, 7] sts, k14 [15, 16] including st used to bind off, turn, leaving rem sts on a holder.
Work each side separately:
Next row (WS): Dec 1 st at neck edge, p to end.
Next row (RS): Bind off 6 [6, 7] sts, k to end.
Next row (WS): Dec 1 st at neck edge, p to end.
Next row (RS): Bind off rem 6 [7, 7] sts.
With RS facing, slip center 24 [26, 26] sts onto a holder for neck edge, rejoin yarn and complete to match first side, reversing shaping.

FRONT
Work as for back to armhole shaping, positioning and knitting the dog as instructed for your chosen dog breed (see index of dogs, page 140).
SHAPE ARMHOLES:
Bind off 6 [7, 8] sts at beg of next 2 rows. (64 [68, 72] sts)
Continue straight until armhole measures 2 [2, 2¼] in/5 [5, 6] cm, ending on a p row.
SHAPE FRONT NECK:
With RS facing, k25 [26, 28], turn, leaving rem sts on a holder.
Work each side separately:
Dec 1 st at neck edge of every row 4 times, and then at neck edge of every other row 3 times. (18 [19, 21] sts)

Continue straight until front matches back at shoulder, ending on a p row.

SHAPE SHOULDERS:
Next row (RS): Bind off 6 [6, 7] sts, k to end.
Next row (WS): Purl.
Next row (RS): Bind off 6 [6, 7] sts.
Next row (WS): Purl.
Next row (RS): Bind off rem 6 [7, 7] sts.
With RS facing, slip center 14 [16, 16] sts onto a holder, rejoin yarn and k to end. Complete to match first side, reversing shaping.

SLEEVES (MAKE 2)
With US 3/3.25mm needles, cast on 42 [44, 46] sts and work rib as for back. Change to US 6/4mm needles.

Beg with a k row, continue in st st, shaping sides by inc 1 st at each end of next and every following 6th row 12 [12, 10] times, and then at each end of every 8th row 0 [0, 3] times. *(66 [68, 72] sts)*
Continue straight until sleeve measures 10¾ [11¾, 13] in/ 27 [30, 33] cm, ending on a p row. Bind off 6 [7, 8] sts at beg of next 2 rows. *(54 [54, 56] sts)*
Bind off rem sts.

FINISHING
Block each piece and, using a warm iron and cloth, press all parts except ribbing. Sew in ends. Using backstitch or mattress stitch, sew right shoulder together.

NECK BAND:
With US 3/3.25mm needles and mc and RS facing, starting at left front shoulder pick up 17 [17, 19] sts down left front neck shaping, 14 [16, 16] sts across center front, 17 [17, 19] sts up right front neck shaping, 5 sts down right back shaping, 34 [36, 36] sts across back neck and 5 sts up left back shaping. *(82 [86, 90] sts)*
Work 6 rows k1, p1 rib.
Bind off loosely in rib.

Using backstitch or mattress stitch, sew left shoulder together and neck edge. Set in sleeves and sew up side and sleeve seams. Press with a damp cloth.

BABY'S RAGLAN PULLOVER

FINISHED MEASUREMENTS

Small
To fit age: 6–12 months
Chest: 10in/25cm
To fit chest: 17¼in/44cm
Length: 10in/25cm

Medium
To fit age: 1–2 years
Chest: 11in/28cm
To fit chest: 19in/48cm
Length: 11½in/29cm

Large
To fit age: 2–3 years
Chest: 12¼in/31cm
To fit chest: 21in/53cm
Length: 12½in/32cm

NEEDLES AND YARN
- US 3/3.25mm knitting needles
- US 6/4mm knitting needles
- Main color (mc): Erika Knight British Blue Wool or Erika Knight British Blue 100 (CYCA #3)

Size	Small	Medium	Large
Quantity	120g (4¼oz)	145g (5oz)	175g (6oz)

- 10g (¼oz) of Erika Knight yarn in contrast color (optional)

GAUGE
22 sts and 30 rows to 4in/10cm measured over st st using US 6/4mm needles

DOG ON FRONT
All of the dogs are different shapes and colors. For yarn requirements and knitting instructions, refer to the index of dogs on page 140. This will direct you to the instructions and chart for your chosen breed.

BACK
With US 3/3.25mm needles and mc, cast on 58 [64, 70] sts.
Work 6 [6, 8] rows k1, p1 rib.
NOTE: For version with contrast edge, use contrast yarn to cast on and work first rib row, then change to mc to complete rib.
Change to US 6/4mm needles.
Beg with a k row, continue in st st until back measures 6½ [7, 8] in/ 16.5 [18, 20] cm, ending on a p row.
SHAPE ARMHOLES:
Bind off 4 [4, 5] sts at beg of next 2 rows. (50 [56, 60] sts)
Dec 1 st at each end of next and every other row 13 [16, 17] times, ending on a p row. (24 [24, 26] sts)

Leave rem 24 [24, 26] sts on a holder for neck edge.

FRONT
Work as for back to armhole shaping, positioning and knitting the dog as instructed for your chosen dog breed (see index of dogs, page 140).
SHAPE ARMHOLES:
Bind off 4 [4, 5] sts at beg of next 2 rows. (50 [56, 60] sts)
Dec 1 st at each end of next and every other row 8 [10, 11] times, ending on a p row. (34 [36, 38] sts)
SHAPE FRONT NECK:
With RS facing, k2tog, k9 [10, 11], turn, leaving rem sts on a holder.
Work each side separately:

Dec 1 st at neck edge of next 2 rows, and then at neck edge of every other row 2 [2, 3] times, and **at the same time** continue raglan shaping by dec 1 st at armhole edge of every other row until 2 sts remain, ending on a p row, then k2tog and fasten off.
With RS facing, slip center 12 sts onto a holder for neck edge, rejoin yarn and k to last 2 sts, k2tog.
Complete to match first side, reversing shaping.

SLEEVES (MAKE 2)

With US 3/3.25mm needles, cast on 34 [36, 40] sts and work rib as for back.

Change to US 6/4mm needles.

Next row (RS): K2, inc, k28 [30, 34], inc, k2. *(36 [38, 42] sts)*

Beg with a p row, continue in st st, shaping sides by inc 1 st as set at each end of every 8th [6th, 6th] row 5 [7, 7] times. *(46 [52, 56] sts)*

Continue straight until sleeve measures 7 [8, 8¾] in/18 [20, 22] cm, ending on a p row.

SHAPE SLEEVE TOP:

Bind off 4 [4, 5] sts at beg of next 2 rows. *(38 [44, 46] sts)*

Dec 1 st at each end of next and every other row 13 [16, 17] times, ending on a p row. *(12 sts)*

Leave rem 12 sts on a holder for neck edge.

FINISHING

Block each piece and, using a warm iron and cloth, press all parts except ribbing. Sew in ends. Using backstitch or mattress stitch, sew up raglan seams but leave left back raglan open.

NECK BAND:

With US 3/3.25mm needles and mc and RS facing, pick up 12 sts across top of left sleeve, 11 [13, 14] sts down left front neck shaping, 12 sts across center front, 11 [13, 14] sts up right front neck shaping, 12 sts across top of right sleeve and 24 [24, 26] sts across back neck. *(82 [86, 90] sts)*

Work 5 rows k1, p1 rib.

Bind off loosely in rib.

Using backstitch or mattress stitch, sew up remaining raglan seam and neck edge. Sew up side and sleeve seams. Press with a damp cloth.

BABY'S CARDIGAN

FINISHED MEASUREMENTS

Small
To fit age: 0–3 months
Chest: 7½in/19cm
Length: 9in/23cm

Medium
To fit age: 3–6 months
Chest: 8¾in/22cm
Length: 10¼in/26cm

NEEDLES, YARN AND MATERIALS

- US 3/3.25mm knitting needles
- US 6/4mm knitting needles
- Main color (mc): Erika Knight British Blue Wool or Erika Knight British Blue 100 (CYCA #3)

Size	Small	Medium
Quantity	90g (3¼oz)	110g (4oz)

- 10g (¼oz) of Erika Knight yarn in contrast color (optional):
  Miniature Schnauzer: Mouse (grey – mu)
  Dachshund: Mrs Dalloway (ochre – oc)
  Jack Russell: Milk Chocolate (me)
- 6 [7] small buttons

GAUGE
22 sts and 30 rows to 4in/10cm measured over st st using US 6/4mm needles

DOGS ON FRONT
Erika Knight British Blue Wool or Erika Knight British Blue 100 in the following colors:
Miniature Schnauzer: 5g (⅛oz) of Mouse (grey – mu), 5g (⅛oz) of Pitch (black – bl), 5g (⅛oz) of Rowan Kidsilk Haze (CYCA #3) in 00634 Cream (mohair – mo) – use THREE strands of mo together throughout
Dachshund: 5g (⅛oz) of Pitch (black – bl), 5g (⅛oz) of Mrs Dalloway (ochre – oc)
Jack Russell: 5g (⅛oz) of Milk (cream – cr), 5g (⅛oz) of Milk Chocolate (me), small amount of Pitch (black – bl) for eye and nose. For picture see page 100.

CHARTS
See page 136

NOTE: Work eyebrows of Miniature Schnauzer using THREE strands of mo together and loopy stitch (see page 75).

BACK

With US 3/3.25mm needles and mc, cast on 44 [50] sts.

Row 1 (RS): [K1, p1] to end.

Row 2: [P1, k1] to end.

These 2 rows set seed st.

Repeat rows 1–2 twice more.

(6 rows in total)

NOTE: For version with contrast edge, use contrast yarn to cast on and work first seed st row, then change to mc to complete hem.

Change to US 6/4mm needles.

Beg with a k row, continue in st st until back measures 4¾ [5½] in/ 12 [14] cm, ending on a p row.

SHAPE ARMHOLES:

Bind off 3 [4] sts at beg of next 2 rows, and then 1 st at each end of next and every other row 3 times. *(32 [36] sts)*

Continue straight until armhole measures 4¼ [4¾] in/11 [12] cm, ending on a p row.

SHAPE SHOULDERS:

Bind off 7 [8] sts at beg of next 2 rows.

Leave rem 18 [20] sts on a holder for neck edge.

POCKET BACK (MAKE 2)

With US 6/4mm needles and mc, cast on 14 sts.

Beg with a k row, work 14 rows st st.

Leave 14 sts on a holder.

LEFT FRONT

With US 3/3.25mm needles and mc, cast on 22 [24] sts and work 6 rows seed st as for back, inc 0 [1] st on last row. *(22 [25] sts)*

Change to US 6/4mm needles.

Beg with a k row, work 14 rows st st. Cut yarn.

Pocket top: Slip 4 [5] sts onto a holder, rejoin mc, then on next 14 sts only with US 3/3.25mm needles, work 3 rows seed st and then bind off.

With US 6/4mm needles and mc and beg with a k row, k4 [5] from holder, replace bound-off sts with 14 sts from pocket back and begin chart for your chosen dog as follows:

Jack Russell: K5mc, k2cr, k7mc, continue in mc and k4 [6].

Miniature Schnauzer: K5mc, k4mu, k5mc, continue in mc and k4 [6].

Dachshund: K2mc, k2bl, k1mc, k2bl, k7mc, continue in mc and k4 [6].

Continue chart pattern until dog is finished and then continue in mc and st st, and **at the same time** shape armhole when front measures 4¾ [5½] in/12 [14] cm, ending on a p row.

SHAPE ARMHOLE:

Bind off 3 [4] sts at beg of next row, then dec 1 st at armhole edge on every other row 3 times. *(16 [18] sts)*

Continue until armhole measures 2¼in/6cm, ending on a p row.

SHAPE FRONT NECK:

With RS facing, k12 [14], turn, leaving rem 4 sts on a holder.

Dec 1 st at neck edge of every row 3 [4] times, and then at neck edge of every other row twice. *(7 [8] sts)*

Continue straight until armhole measures 4¼ [4¾] in/11 [12] cm, ending on a p row.

Bind off.

RIGHT FRONT

Work as for left front to pocket top.

Pocket top: Slip 4 [6] sts onto a holder, rejoin mc, then on next 14 sts only with US 3/3.25mm needles, work 3 rows seed st and then bind off.

With US 6/4mm needles and mc and beg with a k row, k4 [6] from holder, replace bound-off sts with 14 sts from pocket back and begin chart for your chosen dog as follows:

Jack Russell: K7mc, k2cr, k5mc, continue in mc and k4 [5].

Miniature Schnauzer: K5mc, k4mu, k5mc, continue in mc and k4 [5].

Dachshund: K7mc, k2bl, k1mc, k2bl, k2mc, continue in mc and k4 [5].

Continue chart pattern until dog is finished and then continue in mc and st st, and **at the same time** shape armhole when front measures 4¾ [5½] in/12 [14] cm, ending on a k row.

SHAPE ARMHOLE:

Bind off 3 [4] sts at beg of next row, then dec 1 st at armhole edge of next and every other row 3 times. *(16 [18] sts)*

Continue until armhole measures 2¼in/6cm, ending on a p row.

SHAPE FRONT NECK:

With RS facing, k4, leave these 4 sts on a holder, k to end. *(12 [14] sts)*
Dec 1 st at neck edge of every row 3 [4] times, and then at neck edge of every other row twice. *(7 [8] sts)*
Continue straight until armhole measures 4¼ [4¾] in/11 [12] cm, ending on a k row.
Bind off.

SLEEVES (MAKE 2)

With US 3/3.25mm needles, cast on 28 [32] sts and work 6 rows seed st as for back.
Change to US 6/4mm needles.
Next row (RS): K2, inc, k22 [26], inc, k2. *(30 [34] sts)*
Beg with a p row, continue in st st, shaping sides by inc 1 st as set at each end of every 6th row twice, and then at each end of every 8th row twice. *(38 [42] sts)*
Continue straight until sleeve measures 6 [6¼] in/15 [16] cm, ending on a p row.

SHAPE SLEEVE TOP:

Bind off 3 [4] sts at beg of next 2 rows, and then 1 st at each end of next and every other row 3 times, ending on a p row. *(26 [28] sts)*
Bind off.

FINISHING

Block each piece and, using a warm iron and cloth, press all parts except ribbing. Sew in ends. Using backstitch or mattress stitch, sew shoulders together.

NECK BAND:

With US 3/3.25mm needles and RS facing, skip 4 sts from stitch holder, rejoin mc and pick up 12 [14] sts from right front neck shaping, 18 [20] sts across back neck, 12 [14] sts from left front neck shaping and 4 sts from stitch holder. *(50 [56] sts)*
Work 5 rows seed st.
NOTE: For version with contrast edge, change to contrast color for final row.
Bind off in seed st.

LEFT BUTTONBAND:

With US 3/3.25mm needles and mc and RS facing, starting at neck edge pick up 50 [54] sts along left side of front.
Starting at hem with a WS row, work 4 rows seed st.
NOTE: For version with contrast edge, use contrast color for 2 sts at neck hem edge on each row of buttonband.
Bind off in seed st.

RIGHT BUTTONBAND:

Work to match left buttonband but work row 2 as follows to add buttonholes:
Row 2 (small size only): K1, p1, *k2tog, yo, [k1, p1] 3 times, k1, p2tog, yo, [p1, k1] 3 times, p1; repeat from * once more, k2tog, yo, [k1, p1] 3 times, k2tog, yo, [k1, p1].
Row 2 (medium size only): K1, p1, *k2tog, yo, [k1, p1] 3 times; repeat from * 3 times more, k1, p2tog, yo, [p1, k1] 3 times, p1, k2tog, yo, [k1, p1] twice, k2tog, yo, k1, p1.

Using backstitch or mattress stitch, set in sleeves and sew up side and sleeve seams. Press with a damp cloth. Sew on buttons.
Eyes: With bl, make a 3-loop French knot for each eye.
Nose: With bl, make 1 duplicate stitch for nose.

LOOPY STITCH

The Miniature Schnauzer's eyebrows are worked in loopy stitch. On a knit row, knit one stitch as normal but leave the stitch on the left-hand needle. Bring the yarn from the back to the front between the two needles. Loop the yarn around the index finger of your left hand. Take the yarn between the two needles to the back of the work. Knit the stitch from the left-hand needle as normal. You now have two stitches on the right-hand needle and a loop between them. Pass the first stitch over the second stitch to trap the loop, which is now secure. On a purl row, take the loop to the RS of the knitting and work knit stitches in purl.

West Highland Terrier

PAGE 80

Easy

Dalmatian

PAGE 82

Easy

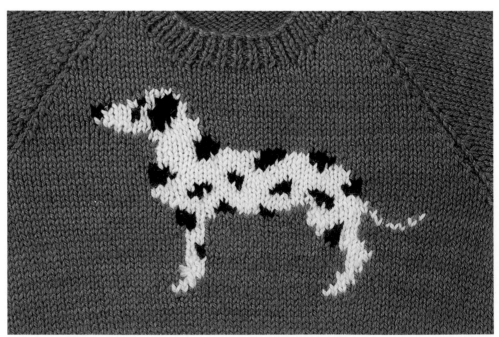

76

Labrador

PAGE 84

Easy

Dachshund

PAGE 86

Intermediate

Pug

PAGE 88

Easy

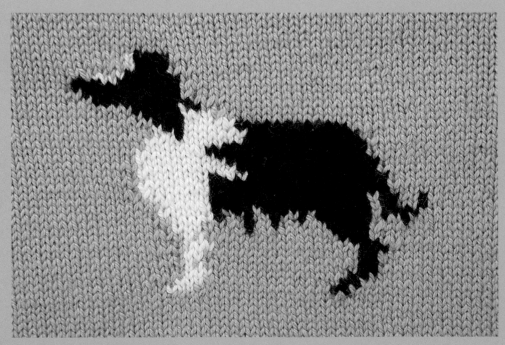

Border Collie

PAGE 90

Easy

Jack Russell

PAGE 92

Intermediate

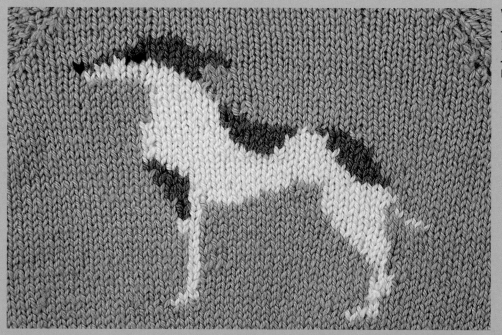

Whippet

PAGE 94

Intermediate

WEST HIGHLAND TERRIER

YARN
- Main color: Erika Knight British Blue Wool (CYCA #3) in Pretty – pale pink (mc)
- 15g (½oz) of Rowan Kidsilk Haze (CYCA #2) in Cream (mohair – mo) – use THREE strands together throughout
- Tiny amount of Erika Knight British Blue Wool in Pitch – black (bl) for nose and eye
- Small amount of Erika Knight British Blue Wool in French – mauve (fr) for collar

CHART
See page 135

BABY'S RAGLAN PULLOVER
(PAGE 70)
Continue in st st until front measures 3 [4, 5] in/8 [10, 13] cm, ending on a p row.
Follow chart for West Highland Terrier.
Row 1: K15 [18, 21] mc, k4mo, k14mc, k3mo, k22 [25, 28] mc.
Continue chart pattern until dog is finished.

CHILD'S PULLOVER
(PAGE 68)
Continue in st st until front measures 6 [7, 8¾] in/15 [18, 22] cm, ending on a p row.
Follow chart for West Highland Terrier.
Row 1: K24 [27, 30] mc, k4mo, k14mc, k3mo, k31 [34, 37] mc.
Continue chart pattern until dog is finished.

FINISHING DETAILS
Eye: With bl, make a 3-loop French knot for eye.
Collar: With US 6/4mm needles and fr, cast on 20 sts and knit 1 row. Bind off. Push each end into the side of the dog's neck, and sew collar ends together on reverse side of pullover.

DALMATIAN

YARN
- Main color: Erika Knight British Blue 100 (CYCA #3) in Ballet Russes – bright pink (mc)
- 10g (¼oz) of Erika Knight British Blue Wool (CYCA #3) in Milk – cream (cr)
- 5g (⅛oz) of Erika Knight British Blue Wool in Pitch – black (bl)

CHART
See page 133

BABY'S RAGLAN PULLOVER (PAGE 70)
Continue in st st until front measures 3 [4¼, 5½] in/8 [11, 14] cm, ending on a p row.
Follow chart for Dalmatian.
Row 1: K19 [22, 25] mc, k2cr, k17mc, k2cr, k18 [21, 24] mc.
Continue chart pattern until dog is finished.

CHILD'S PULLOVER (PAGE 68)
Continue in st st until front measures 5½ [7, 8¾] in/14 [18, 22] cm, ending on a p row.
Follow chart for Dalmatian.
Row 1: K28 [31, 34] mc, k2cr, k17mc, k2cr, k27 [30, 33] mc.
Continue chart pattern until dog is finished.

LABRADOR

YARN
- Main color: Erika Knight British Blue Wool (CYCA #3) in Milk – cream (mc)
- 10g (¼oz) of Erika Knight British Blue Wool in Pitch – black (bl)
- Small amount of DK-weight yarn in brown (br) for eye

CHART
See page 134

BABY'S RAGLAN PULLOVER (PAGE 70)
Continue in st st until front measures 3 [4¼, 5½] in/8 [11, 14] cm, ending on a p row.
Follow chart for Labrador.
Row 1: K19 [22, 25] mc, k2bl, k17mc, k2bl, k18 [21, 24] mc.
Continue chart pattern until dog is finished.

CHILD'S PULLOVER (PAGE 68)
Continue in st st until front measures 5½ [7, 8¾] in/14 [18, 22] cm, ending on a p row.
Follow chart for Labrador.
Row 1: K28 [31, 34] mc, k2bl, k17mc, k2bl, k27 [30, 33] mc.
Continue chart pattern until dog is finished.

FINISHING DETAILS
Eye: With br, make a 3-loop French knot for eye.

DACHSHUND

YARN AND MATERIALS

- Main color: Erika Knight British Blue 100 (CYCA #3) in French – mauve (mc)
- Contrast stripe: 20g (¾oz) of Erika Knight British Blue Wool (CYCA #3) in Milk – cream (cr)
- 10g (¼oz) of Erika Knight British Blue Wool in Pitch – black (bl)
- 5g (⅛oz) of Erika Knight British Blue 100 in Mrs Dalloway – ochre (oc)
- Black bead for eye, plus sewing needle and black thread for sewing on (optional)

CHART

See page 132

CHILD'S PULLOVER (PAGE 68)

Because of its length, the Dachshund is suitable for a child-size sweater only. Our Dachshund is knitted on a contrast stripe. Continue in st st until front measures 8¼ [10¼, 12¼] in/ 21 [26, 31] cm, ending on a p row.

NOTE: For version without a contrast stripe, work first and last bl rows and all cr sts in mc.

START STRIPE:

Work 1 row in bl and then 3 rows in cr, ending on a p row.

Follow chart for Dachshund.

Row 5: K24 [27, 30] cr, k1bl, k1oc, k21cr, k1bl, k1oc, k27 [30, 33] cr.

Continue chart pattern until dog is finished, ending on a k row.

Work 3 rows in cr and then 1 row in bl, ending on a k row.

Continue in mc.

FINISHING DETAILS

Eye: Sew on bead for eye, just below eyebrow stitch (optional).

PUG

YARN

- Main color: Erika Knight British Blue Wool (CYCA #3) in Mr Bhasin – petrol (mc)
- 10g (¼oz) of Erika Knight British Blue Wool in Fawn (fn)
- 5g (⅛oz) of Erika Knight British Blue Wool in Pitch – black (bl)
- Tiny amount of Erika Knight British Blue Wool in Milk – cream (cr) for eye

CHART

See page 134

BABY'S RAGLAN PULLOVER (PAGE 70)

Continue in st st until front measures 3½ [4¼, 5½] in/9 [11, 14] cm, ending on a p row.
Follow chart for Pug.
Row 1: K17 [20, 23] mc, k3fn, k12mc, k3fn, k23 [26, 29] mc.
Continue chart pattern until dog is finished.

CHILD'S PULLOVER (PAGE 68)

Continue in st st until front measures 6 [7, 8¾] in/15 [18, 22] cm, ending on a p row.
Follow chart for Pug.
Row 1: K26 [29, 32] mc, k3fn, k12mc, k3fn, k32 [35, 38] mc.
Continue chart pattern until dog is finished.

FINISHING DETAILS

Eyes: With bl, make a 3-loop French knot for each eye and sew a small slanting stitch above each eye in cr.

BORDER COLLIE

YARN AND MATERIALS

- Main color: Erika Knight British Blue Wool (CYCA #3) in Iced Gem – aqua (mc)
- 10g (¼oz) of Erika Knight British Blue Wool in Milk – cream (cr)
- 10g (¼oz) of Erika Knight British Blue Wool in Pitch – black (bl)
- Black bead for eye, plus sewing needle and black thread for sewing on (optional – child's pullover only)

CHART

See page 132

BABY'S RAGLAN PULLOVER (PAGE 70)

Continue in st st until front measures 3 [4¼, 5½] in/8 [11, 14] cm, ending on a p row.

Follow chart for Border Collie.

Row 1: K19 [22, 25] mc, k3bl, k14mc, k2cr, k20 [23, 26] mc.

Continue chart pattern until dog is finished.

CHILD'S PULLOVER (PAGE 68)

Continue in st st until front measures 6 [7, 8¾] in/15 [18, 22] cm, ending on a p row.

Follow chart for Border Collie.

Row 1: K28 [31, 34] mc, k2bl, k14mc, k3cr, k29 [32, 35] mc.

Continue chart pattern until dog is finished.

FINISHING DETAILS

Eye: On child's pullover only, sew on bead for eye (optional).

JACK RUSSELL

YARN
- Main color: Erika Knight British Blue Wool (CYCA #3) in Mouse – grey (mc)
- Contrast color (child's pullover only): 20g (¾oz) of Erika Knight British Blue 100 (CYCA #3) in Kanoko – pale blue (pb)
- 10g (¼oz) of Erika Knight British Blue Wool in Milk – cream (cr)
- 5g (⅛oz) of Erika Knight British Blue Wool in Milk Chocolate (me)
- Small amount of Erika Knight British Blue Wool in 4002 Pitch – black (bl) for eye and nose

CHART
See page 133

BABY'S RAGLAN PULLOVER (PAGE 70)
This is an example for knitting the Jack Russell without an oval.
Continue in st st until front measures 3 [4¼, 5½] in/8 [11, 14] cm, ending on a p row.
Follow chart for Jack Russell.
Row 1: K19 [22, 25] mc, k2cr, k17mc, k2cr, k18 [21, 24] mc.
Continue chart pattern until dog is finished.

CHILD'S PULLOVER (PAGE 68)
Our Jack Russell is knitted on a contrast oval. Continue in st st until front measures 4¾ [6¼, 8] in/ 12 [16, 20] cm, ending on a p row.
NOTE: For version without a contrast oval, work all pb sts in mc.
Follow chart for Jack Russell in oval.
Row 1: K34 [37, 40] mc, k8pb, k34 [37, 40] mc.
Continue to follow chart for oval.
START OF JACK RUSSELL:
Row 7: K22 [25, 28] mc, k4pb, k2cr, k17pb, k2cr, k7pb, k22 [25, 28] mc.
Continue chart pattern until dog and oval are finished.
Continue in mc.

FINISHING DETAILS
Eye: With bl, make a 3-loop French knot for eye.
Nose: With bl, make 1 duplicate stitch for nose.

WHIPPET

YARN
- Main color: Erika Knight British Blue 100 (CYCA #3) in Kanoko – pale blue (mc)
- 10g (¼oz) of Erika Knight British Blue Wool (CYCA #3) in Milk – cream (cr)
- 5g (⅛oz) of Erika Knight British Blue Wool in Mouse – grey (mu)
- Tiny amount of Erika Knight British Blue Wool in Pitch – black (bl) for nose and eye

CHART
See page 135

BABY'S RAGLAN PULLOVER (PAGE 70)
Continue in st st until front measures 2¾ [4, 5] in/7 [10, 13] cm, ending on a p row.
Follow chart for Whippet.
Row 1: K17 [20, 23] mc, k2cr, k17mc, k2cr, k20 [23, 26] mc.
Continue chart pattern until dog is finished.

CHILD'S PULLOVER (PAGE 68)
Continue in st st until front measures 5½ [7, 8¾] in/14 [18, 22] cm, ending on a p row.
Follow chart for Whippet.
Row 1: K26 [29, 32] mc, k2cr, k17mc, k2cr, k29 [32, 35] mc.
Continue chart pattern until dog is finished.

FINISHING DETAILS
Eye: With bl, make a 3-loop French knot for eye.

ACCESSORIES

We have included a mixture of adult, child and dog accessories; all of the accessories are pictured on pages 98–99 to help you make your selection. The Pug Hat and Jack Russell Scarf are both for adults. If you want, you can choose another dog breed – most of the charts will fit (the index of dogs on page 140 lists the stitch and row dimensions of each dog breed). The adorable Pug, Jack Russell and Dachshund Booties are for babies aged 3–6 months. The spectacular Dalmatian Onesie is for babies aged 3–6 months and 6–12 months. The Patchwork Baby Blanket can be customized to suit the child, and is the perfect present to hand down from generation to generation. The Dog Coat is knitted in worsted-weight yarn. All the adult sweaters are also knitted in worsted yarn, so you and your dog can complement one another.

Pug hat

PAGE 100

Dalmatian onesie

PAGE 102

Dachshund booties

PAGE 106

Pug booties

PAGE 108

Jack Russell booties

PAGE 111

Jack Russell scarf

PAGE 110

Patchwork baby blanket

PAGE 114

Dog coat

PAGE 112

PUG HAT

FINISHED MEASUREMENTS
To fit average-size adult head
Length: 11¾in/30cm

LEVEL
Intermediate

NEEDLES AND YARN
- US 3/3.25mm knitting needles
- US 6/4mm knitting needles
- 80g (2¾oz) of Erika Knight British Blue Wool (CYCA #3) in French – mauve (mc)
- 15g (½oz) of Erika Knight British Blue Wool in Fawn (fn)
- Tiny amount of Erika Knight British Blue Wool in Pitch – black (bl)

GAUGE
11 sts and 15 rows to 2in/5cm measured over st st using US 6/4mm needles

CHART
See page 134 for Pug (child size)

HAT
With US 3/3.25mm needles and mc, cast on 108 sts.
Work k2, p2 rib for 2¾in/7cm.
Change to US 6/4mm needles.
Beg with a k row, continue in st st until work measures 4¾in/12cm, ending on a p row.
Follow chart for Pug, placing dog in center of hat.
Row 1 of dog: K48mc, k3fn, k12mc, k3fn, k42mc.
Continue chart pattern until dog is finished and work measures 11in/28cm, ending on a p row.

SHAPE TOP OF HAT:
Next row: K2tog, [k10, k2tog] 8 times, k8, k2tog. (98 sts)
Next row: Purl.
Next row: K2tog, [k9, k2tog] 8 times, k6, k2tog. (88 sts)
Next row: Purl.
Next row: K2tog, [k8, k2tog] 8 times, k4, k2tog. (78 sts)
Next row: Purl.
Next row: K2tog, [k7, k2tog] 8 times, k2, k2tog. (68 sts)
Next row: Purl.
Next row: K2tog, [k6, k2tog] 8 times, k2. (59 sts)
Next row: Purl.
Bind off.

FINISHING
Sew up side seam using mattress stitch for rib and whipstitch for remainder. Sew in ends.

DALMATIAN ONESIE

FINISHED MEASUREMENTS

Small

To fit age: 3–6 months

Length to shoulder: 22in/56cm

Chest: 13in/33cm

Sleeves to armpit: 6¼in/16cm

Medium

To fit age: 6–12 months

Length to shoulder: 23½in/60cm

Chest: 15in/38cm

Sleeves to armpit: 7in/18cm

LEVEL

Difficult

NEEDLES AND YARN

- US 6/4mm knitting needles
- US 8/5mm knitting needles
- Cascade 220 in 8505 White (wh)

Size	Small	Medium
Quantity	325g (11½oz)	350g (12½oz)

- 50g (2oz) of Cascade 220 in 8555 Black (bl)
- 6 black buttons

GAUGE

18 sts and 24 rows to 4in/10cm measured over st st using US 8/5mm needles

CHARTS

See pages 137 and 138

NOTE: Work odd-numbered rows on the charts as knit (read from right to left) and even-numbered rows as purl (read from left to right). Use the Fair Isle method (see page 9) for working Dalmatian spots over the whole of the st st sections of the legs, body, hood and sleeves of the onesie.

LEGS (MAKE 4 PIECES)

Left back leg: With US 6/4mm needles and wh, cast on 18 [20] sts.
Work 10 rows k1, p1 rib.
Change to US 8/5mm needles.
Beg with a k row and working spot pattern from chart 1, continue in st st.
Work 34 [40] rows, inc 1 st on outer edge (beg) of every 8th [10th] row 4 [3] times, and **at the same time** inc 1 st on inside leg (end) of every 6th [4th] row 5 [7] times. *(27 [30] sts)*
Leave rem sts on a holder for back.
Right front leg: Work as for left back leg.
Left front leg: Work as for left back leg but reverse shaping.
Right back leg: Work as for left back leg but reverse shaping.
NOTE: The increase on every 6th [4th] row should be on the inside of all four leg pieces.

BACK

With US 8/5mm needles and wh and RS facing, k27 [30] sts from holder for right back leg, then k27 [30] sts from holder for left back leg (inner leg increases should be in center of this needle). *(54 [60] sts)*
Beg with a p row and continuing spot pattern from chart 2 row 2, continue in st st.
Inc 1 st at each end of every following 8th [10th] row from previous inc 4 [5] times. *(62 [70] sts)*

Continue straight until back measures 15¾ [17] in/40 [43] cm, ending on a p row.

SHAPE ARMHOLES:

Bind off 3 sts at each end of next 2 rows, then dec 1 st at each end of next and every other row 4 [5] times. *(48 [54] sts)*
Continue straight until armhole measures 6¼ [6¾] in/16 [17] cm, ending on a k row.
Bind off 12 [14] sts, p24 [26] including st used to bind off, leave center 24 [26] sts on a holder for back of hood, then bind off rem sts.

FRONT

With US 8/5mm needles and wh and RS facing, k27 [30] sts from holder for left front leg, then k27 [30] sts from holder for right front leg (inner leg increases should be in center of this needle). *(54 [60] sts)*
Beg with a p row and continuing spot pattern from chart 2 row 2, work in st st for 1¼in/3cm, ending on a p row (there will be one inc at each end of one row in this section). *(56 [62] sts)*

DIVIDE FOR FRONT OPENING:

With RS facing, k26 [29], turn, leaving rem 30 [33] sts on a holder for right front.
Working on 26 [29] sts for left front, continue in st st, inc 1 st on outer edge of every 8th [10th] row 3 [4] times. *(29 [33] sts)*

Continue straight until left front measures 15¾ [17] in/40 [43] cm, ending on a p row.

SHAPE ARMHOLE:

Bind off 3 sts at beg of next row, and then 1 st at armhole edge of every other row 4 [5] times. *(22 [25] sts)*
Continue straight until armhole measures 4¾ [5] in/12 [13] cm, ending on a p row.

SHAPE FRONT NECK:

K17 [20], leaving rem 5 sts on holder for center front neck.
Dec 1 st at neck edge of every row 3 [4] times, and then 1 st at neck edge of every other row twice. *(12 [14] sts)*
Continue until armhole measures 6¼ [6¾] in/16 [17] cm, ending on a p row.
Bind off for shoulder.
Working on 30 [33] sts from holder for right front, bind off 4 sts and then complete to match left front, reversing all shaping.

BACK AND TOP OF HOOD

With US 8/5mm needles and RS facing, rejoin yarns and pattern 24 [26] sts from holder for back of hood.
Beg with a p row and continuing spot pattern from chart 1, work in st st for 8¼ [9] in/21 [23] cm.
Leave sts on a holder for buttonband.

SIDES OF HOOD
(MAKE 2 PIECES)
Left side: With US 8/5mm needles and wh, cast on 10 sts.

Beg with a k row and working spot pattern from chart 1, work 2 rows st st.

Then inc 1 st at beg (back edge) of next and every row 12 times. *(22 sts)*

Continue straight until left side of hood measures 5½ [6¼] in/ 14 [16] cm, measured at the longer edge, ending on a p row.

Dec 1 st at beg of next and every other row 5 times. *(17 sts)*

Bind off.

Right side: Work as for left side but reverse all shaping.

SLEEVES (MAKE 2)
With US 6/4mm needles and wh, cast on 30 [32] sts.

Work 10 rows k1, p1 rib.

Change to US 8/5mm needles.

Beg with a k row and working spot pattern from chart 1, continue in st st.

Inc 1 st at each end of next and every following 4th row 7 times. *(44 [46] sts)*

Continue straight until sleeve measures 6¼ [7] in/16 [18] cm, ending on a p row.

SHAPE SLEEVE TOP:
Bind off 3 sts beg of next 2 rows, then dec 1 st at each end of next and every other row 4 times. *(30 [32] sts)*

Bind off.

FINISHING
Block each piece and, using a warm iron and cloth, press all parts except ribbing. Sew in ends. Using backstitch or mattress stitch, sew shoulders together. Sew right side of hood to right front of body, and sew left side of hood to left front of body. Sew up hood in preparation for adding the buttonbands.

RIGHT BUTTONBAND:
With US 6/4mm needles and wh, pick up 100 [110] sts from crotch of right front to center of hood.

Work 5 rows k1, p1 rib.

Bind off.

LEFT BUTTONBAND:
Work to match right buttonband but work row 3 as follows to add buttonholes:

Row 3: [K1, p1] 1 [2] times, *k2tog, yo, [k1, p1] 4 times; repeat from * 5 times, k2tog, yo, rib to end.

EARS (MAKE 2):
With US 6/4mm needles and bl, cast on 3 sts.

Knit 2 rows.

Continue in garter st, inc 1 st at each end of next and every other row 3 times. *(9 sts)*

Knit 8 rows.

Bind off.

Using backstitch or mattress stitch, set in sleeves and sew up leg, sleeve and side seams. Sew bottom of buttonbands to bound-off 4 sts on front. Join bound-off edges at center top. Sew ears to side seams of hood at curve. Press with a damp cloth. Sew on buttons.

DACHSHUND BOOTIES

FINISHED MEASUREMENTS
To fit age: 3–6 months
Length: 4¾in/12cm

LEVEL
Intermediate

NEEDLES AND YARN
- US 3/3.25mm knitting needles
- 15g (½oz) of Erika Knight British Blue Wool (CYCA #3) in Pitch – black (bl)
- 5g (⅛oz) of Erika Knight British Blue 100 (CYCA #3) in Mrs Dalloway – ochre (oc)

GAUGE
12 sts and 17 rows to 2in/5cm measured over st st

BOOTIES (MAKE 2)
With bl, cast on 26 sts.
Row 1: Knit.
Row 2: K4, p18, k4.
Rep rows 1–2, 10 times more.
Join in oc.
Row 23: K6bl, k14oc, k6bl.
Row 24: P3bl, p2oc, p1bl, p14oc, p1bl, p2oc, p3bl.
Row 25: K2togbl, k1bl, k2oc, k1bl, k14oc, k1bl, k2oc, k1bl, k2togbl. *(24 sts)*
Row 26: P6bl, p12oc, p6bl.
Row 27: K2togbl, k4bl, k12oc, k4bl, k2togbl. *(22 sts)*
Row 28: P5bl, p12oc, p5bl.
Row 29: K2togbl, k3bl, k12oc, k3bl, k2togbl. *(20 sts)*
Row 30: P5bl, p10oc, p5bl.
Row 31: K2togbl, k3bl, k10oc, k3bl, k2togbl. *(18 sts)*
Row 32: P4bl, p10oc, p4bl.
Row 33: K2togbl, k2bl, k10oc, k2bl, k2togbl. *(16 sts)*
Row 34: P4bl, p8oc, p4bl.
Row 35: K2togbl, k2bl, k8oc, k2bl, k2togbl. *(14 sts)*

Row 36: P3bl, p8oc, p3bl.
Row 37: K2togbl, k1bl, k8oc, k1bl, k2togbl. *(12 sts)*
Row 38: P3bl, p6oc, p3bl.
Bind off in bl.

EARS (MAKE 4)
With bl, cast on 6 sts.
Work 4 rows garter st.
Row 5: Inc, k4, inc. *(8 sts)*
Work 3 rows garter st.
Row 9: Inc, k6, inc. *(10 sts)*
Work 5 rows garter st.
Row 15: K2tog, k6, k2tog. *(8 sts)*
Work 3 rows garter st.
Row 19: K2tog, k4, k2tog. *(6 sts)*
Bind off.

TAIL (MAKE 2)
With bl, cast on 12 sts.
Bind off.

FINISHING
For each bootie, sew up back seam. Fold bootie in half and sew up center front seam to where garter st edge finishes – approx 2¾in/7cm.
Ears: Sew cast-on edge of ears to bootie, one on either side of seam at top edge.
Tail: Sew tail to center back seam, facing upwards.
Sew in all ends.

PUG BOOTIES

FINISHED MEASUREMENTS
To fit age: 3–6 months
Length: 4in/10cm

LEVEL
Intermediate

NEEDLES AND YARN
- US 3/3.25mm knitting needles
- US 2/2.75mm knitting needles
- 15g (½oz) of Erika Knight British Blue Wool (CYCA #3) in Fawn (fn)
- 10g (¼oz) Erika Knight British Blue Wool in Pitch – black (bl)

GAUGE
10 sts and 20 rows to 2in/5cm measured over garter st using US 3/3.25mm needles

BOOTIES (MAKE 2)
With US 3/3.25mm needles and fn, cast on 26 sts.
Work 30 rows garter st.
Change to bl.
Beg with a k row, continue in st st.
Row 31: K2tog, k22, k2tog. (24 sts)
Row 32: Purl.
Row 33: K2tog, k20, k2tog. (22 sts)
Row 34: Purl.
Row 35: K2tog, k18, k2tog. (20 sts)
Row 36: Purl.
Row 37: K2tog, k16, k2tog. (18 sts)
Row 38: Purl.
Row 39: K2tog, k14, k2tog. (16 sts)
Row 40: Purl.
Row 41: K2tog, k12, k2tog. (14 sts)
Row 42: Purl.
Row 43: K2tog, k10, k2tog. (12 sts)
Work 6 rows st st.
Bind off.

EYES (MAKE 4)
With US 2/2.75mm needles and bl, cast on 1 st.
Row 1: [Knit into front and back of st] twice, then knit into front again. (5 sts)
Beg with a p row, work 4 rows st st.
Bind off.

EARS (MAKE 4)
With US 2/2.75mm needles and bl, cast on 5 sts.
Beg with a k row, work 5 rows st st.
Bind off.

TAIL (MAKE 2)
For each bootie, sew up back seam. With US 3/3.25mm needles and fn and nose of bootie facing, pick up and k2 from either side of back seam. (4 sts)
Beg with a p row, work 14 rows st st.
Bind off.

FINISHING
Fold each bootie in half and sew approx 1in/2.5cm of fn up from bl across instep. Sew along bl seam and down nose. This sewing-up line sits at the top of the bootie.
Nose: Fold back ⅜in/1cm at end of nose (like a jelly roll) and catch down where you have folded at second row of fn. With bl, sew 3 satin stitches (straight, parallel stitches worked closely together) across where you have caught down the nose.
Eyes: Sew on eyes, approx 1 row up from fn and 2 sts across from center seam.
Ears: Sew an ear onto each side of bootie, right side up and parallel with center seam.
Tail: Curl tail outwards and sew down at approx second st from top of center back seam.
Sew in all ends.

109

JACK RUSSELL SCARF

FINISHED MEASUREMENTS
Length: 65¼in/166cm
Width: 9½in/24cm

LEVEL
Easy to intermediate

NEEDLES AND YARN
- US 3/3.25mm knitting needles
- US 6/4mm knitting needles
- 250g (8¾oz) of Erika Knight British Blue Wool (CYCA #3) in French – mauve (mc)
- 15g (½oz) of Erika Knight British Blue Wool in Milk – cream (cr)
- 10g (¼oz) of Erika Knight British Blue Wool in Milk Chocolate (me)
- Tiny amount of Erika Knight British Blue Wool in Pitch – black (bl) for eye and nose

GAUGE
22 sts and 30 rows to 4in/10cm measured over st st using US 6/4mm needles

DOGS ON POCKETS
This scarf is knitted with a Jack Russell (adult size) on each pocket, but you could use any of the dog designs except the Dachshund, which is too long. To choose a different dog, refer to the index of dogs on page 140. This will direct you to the chart for your chosen breed, plus the instructions for knitting the dog onto the front of a pullover, which is where you will find a list of yarn requirements and finishing details for the eyes and nose.

CHART
See page 124 for Jack Russell (adult size)

SCARF
With US 3/3.25mm needles and mc, cast on 53 sts.
Row 1: [K1, p1] to last st, k1.
This row sets seed st.
Repeat this row 7 times more.
(8 rows in total)
Change to US 6/4mm needles.
Next row (RS): [K1, p1] twice, k45, [p1, k1] twice.
Next row (WS): [K1, p1] twice, p45, [p1, k1] twice.
These 2 rows set st st pattern with seed st edge.
Work 4 more rows as set.
Follow chart for Jack Russell, but upside down, starting at the head.

Row 1 of dog: Seed st 4mc, k12mc, k3me, k30mc, seed st 4mc.
Continue as set, following chart pattern until dog is finished.
Work 11 rows as set in mc.
Knit 2 rows to make fold line for first pocket.
Beg with a WS row, work 65¼in/166cm as set, ending with a RS row.
Knit 2 rows to make fold line for second pocket.
Beg with a p row, work 11 rows as set.
Follow chart for Jack Russell, but this time right way up, starting at the legs.
Row 1 of dog: Seed st 4mc, k9mc, k2me, k17mc, k2me, k15mc, seed st 4mc.

Continue as set, following chart pattern until dog is finished.
Work 6 rows as set in mc.
Change to US 3/3.25mm needles.
Work 8 rows seed st.
Bind off.

FINISHING
At each end of scarf, fold up pocket along garter st fold line and sew up side seams across seed st edge to make a pocket. Lightly press.
Eye: With bl, make a 3-loop French knot for eye.

JACK RUSSELL BOOTIES

FINISHED MEASUREMENTS
To fit age: 3–6 months
Length: 3½in/9cm

LEVEL
Intermediate

NEEDLES AND YARN
- US 3/3.25mm knitting needles
- 10g (¼oz) of Erika Knight British Blue Wool (CYCA #3) in Milk – cream (cr)
- 5g (⅛oz) of Erika Knight British Blue Wool in Milk Chocolate (me)
- Tiny amount of Erika Knight British Blue Wool in Pitch – black (bl) for eyes and nose

GAUGE
12 sts and 17 rows to 2in/5cm measured over st st

BOOTIES (MAKE 2)
With cr, cast on 26 sts.
Row 1: Knit.
Row 2: K4, p18, k4.
Rep rows 1–2, 5 times more.
Join in me.
Row 13: K11me, k15cr.
Row 14: K4cr, p10cr, p8me, k4me.
Row 15: K13me, k13cr.
Row 16: K4cr, p9cr, p9me, k4me.
Row 17: K10me, k16cr.
Row 18: K4cr, p7cr, p11me, k4me.
Row 19: K15me, k11cr.
Row 20: K4cr, p7cr, p11me, k4me.
Row 21: K2togme, k13me, k9cr, k2togcr. *(24 sts)*
Row 22: K2togcr, k1cr, p7cr, p11me, k1me, k2togme. *(22 sts)*
Row 23: K2togme, k10me, k8cr, k2togcr. *(20 sts)*
Row 24: K2togcr, p8cr, p8me, k2togme. *(18 sts)*
Row 25: K9me, k9cr.
Row 26: P9cr, p9me.
Bind off in cr.

EARS (MAKE 2 IN CR AND 2 IN ME)
With cr/me, cast on 6 sts.
Work 4 rows garter st.
Row 5: K1, [k2tog] twice, k1. *(4 sts)*
Row 6: [K2tog] twice. *(2 sts)*
Row 7: K2tog and fasten off.

TAIL (MAKE 2)
With cr, cast on 8 sts.
Bind off.

FINISHING
For each bootie, sew up back seam. Fold bootie in half and sew up approx 1in/2.5cm straight up center front seam, then sew up center front seam to 2 rows above where me ends.
Ears: Sew cast-on edge of ears to bootie, one on either side of center seam, 2 rows above where center seam ends. Sew cr ear on cr side, and me ear on me side. Catch down the bound-off edge of each ear.
Eyes: With bl, make a 6-loop French knot for each eye, just below where you have caught down the ears.
Nose: With bl, sew 3 satin stitches (straight, parallel stitches worked closely together) across where the straight part of the center seam meets top of bootie.
Tail: Sew tail to center back seam, facing upwards.
Sew in all ends.

DOG COAT

FINISHED MEASUREMENTS

Extra small (XS)
To fit (for example): Chihuahua
Circumference of coat: 12¾in/32.5cm
Length to turtle neck: 12in/30.5cm

Small (S)
To fit (for example): Jack Russell
Circumference of coat: 15¼in/39cm
Length to turtle neck: 14¾in/37.5cm

Medium (M)
To fit (for example): Border Collie
Circumference of coat: 18in/46cm
Length to turtle neck: 18¾in/47.5cm

Large (L)
To fit (for example): Labrador
Circumference of coat: 24in/61cm
Length to turtle neck: 21¾in/55.5cm

Extra large (XL)
To fit (for example): German Shepherd
Circumference of coat: 27¾in/70.5cm
Length to turtle neck: 24in/61cm

LEVEL
Intermediate

NEEDLES AND YARN
- US 6/4mm knitting needles
- US 7/4.5mm knitting needles if using Debbie Bliss yarn or US 8/5mm needles if using Cascade yarn
- Debbie Bliss Donegal Luxury Tweed Aran (CYCA #4) or Cascade 220 Solids and Heathers (CYCA #4) yarn in main color (mc) and contrast color (co)

Size	XS	S	M	L	XL
Main	50g	60g	85g	120g	160g
color (mc)	(2oz)	(2¼oz)	(3oz)	(4¼oz)	(5½oz)
Contrast	15g	20g	30g	45g	60g
color (co)	(½oz)	(¾oz)	(1¼oz)	(1¾oz)	(2¼oz)

NOTE: Our dog coat was knitted in size small using Debbie Bliss Donegal Luxury Tweed Aran in 53 Meadow (mc) and 15 Charcoal (co)

GAUGE
18 sts and 24 rows to 4in/10cm measured over st st using US 7/4.5mm needles for Debbie Bliss yarn or US 8/5mm needles for Cascade yarn

TOP OF COAT
With US 6/4mm needles and co, cast on 34 [40, 48, 64, 74] sts.
Work 6 rows k1, p1 rib.
Change to larger needles.
Join in mc and continue in st st, working first and last 4 sts in co and st st center in mc as follows:
Next row (RS): [K1, p1] twice in co, m1 in mc, k26 [32, 40, 56, 66] mc, m1 in mc, [k1, p1] twice in co.
(36 [42, 50, 66, 76] sts)

Next row (WS): [K1, p1] twice in co, p28 [34, 42, 58, 68] mc, [k1, p1] twice in co.
Continue to inc in this way on next and every other row 7 [3, 3, 5, 5] times, and then inc 1 st on every 4th row 0 [5, 5, 6, 8] times. *(50 [58, 66, 88, 102] sts)*
This sets pattern of st st center with 4-st rib border along each side.
Continue straight in st st with rib border until top of coat measures

3 [4, 5, 7, 8] in/8 [10, 13, 18, 20] cm.
Continue in mc and st st only (no rib border) until top of coat measures 5½ [7½, 11, 13, 14¼] in/ 14 [19, 28, 33, 36] cm, ending on a p row.
MARK LEG OPENINGS:
Mark each end of last row with a colored thread to indicate beg of leg openings.
Continue in st st until top of coat measures (7¼ [9½, 13, 15, 16½] in/

18.5 [24, 33, 38, 42] cm.
Mark each end of last row with a
colored thread to indicate end
of leg openings.
Continue in st st until top of coat
measures 10 [12¼, 15¾, 17¾, 19¾]
in/25 [31, 40, 45, 50] cm, ending on a
p row.

SHAPE SHOULDERS:
Next row (RS): K12 [14, 16, 22, 23],
k2tog, k22 [26, 30, 40, 52], k2tog, k12
[14, 16, 22, 23]. *(48 [56, 64, 86, 100] sts)*
Next row (WS): Purl.
Continue to dec in this way, working
2 sts less in center panel on next and
every other row 4 [5, 5, 11, 13] times.
(40 [46, 54, 64, 74] sts)
Continue in st st until top of coat
measures 12 [14¾, 18¾, 21¾, 24]
in/30.5 [37.5, 47.5, 55.5, 61] cm,
ending on a p row.
Leave rem sts on a holder.

GUSSET
With US 6/4mm needles and co,
cast on 14 [18, 24, 30, 34] sts.
Work k1, p1 rib until gusset
measures 2¼ [3½, 6, 6, 6¼] in/
6 [9, 15, 15, 16] cm.

MARK LEG OPENINGS:
Mark each end of last row with a
colored thread to indicate beg of leg
openings.
Continue in rib, matching
end of leg openings with top
of coat, until gusset measures
7½ [9½, 11, 12, 15] in/
19 [24, 28, 30.5, 38] cm.
Dec 1 st at each end of next and
every other row 3 [4, 6, 8, 9] times.
(8 [10, 12, 14, 16] sts)
Leave rem sts on a holder.

TURTLE NECK
With US 6/4mm needles and
mc and RS facing, rib across

8 [10, 12, 14, 16] sts from holder
for gusset, then rib across
40 [46, 54, 64, 74] sts from holder for
top of coat. *(48 [56, 66, 78, 90] sts)*
Work k1, p1 rib (matching rib
with gusset) until polo neck
measures 4¼ [4¾, 5, 5, 5½] in/
11 [12, 13, 13, 14] cm.
Change to co.
Work 1 row k1, p1 rib.
Bind off loosely in rib.

LEG BANDS
Join gusset from end of leg
openings to neck.
With US 6/4mm needles and mc, pick
up 24 [26, 26, 26, 30] sts around first

leg opening, between markers.
Work 6 rows k1, p1 rib.
Change to co.
Work 1 row k1, p1 rib.
Bind off loosely in rib.
Repeat for second leg opening.

FINISHING
With RS together and matching leg
openings, sew remaining gusset
sides to top of coat. The cast-on
edge of gusset should meet edge of
rib on top of coat. Sew collar seam,
reversing seam on outside for approx
last 2¼–2½in/6–6.5cm of collar for
turnback. Press gently.

PLAIN SQUARES (MAKE 3)

Cast on 42 sts.

Row 1: [K1, p1] to end.
Row 2: [P1, k1] to end.
Row 3: [K1, p1] to end.
Row 4: P1, k1, p1, k37, p1, k1.
Row 5: K1, p1, k1, p37, k1, p1.
Rows 4–5 set pattern of st st with seed st edges.
Work 52 more rows as set.
(57 rows in total)
Work 3 rows seed st.
Bind off in seed st.

STRIPED SQUARES (MAKE 4)

This square is worked in 4-row stripes of two alternating colors, A and B.
With A, cast on 42 sts.

Row 1: [K1, p1] to end.
Row 2: [P1, k1] to end.
Rows 3–4: Repeat rows 1–2.
Change to B.
Work 4 rows st st with 3 seed sts at each edge (as for plain square). Continue as set, alternating colors every 4 rows and working 13 stripes in total. *(56 rows in total)*
Change to A.
Work 4 rows seed st as rows 1–4.
Bind off in seed st.

GARTER STITCH RIDGE SQUARES (MAKE 3)

This square is worked in two alternating colors, A and B.
With A, cast on 42 sts and work rows 1–5 as for plain square.
Rows 4–5 set pattern of st st with seed st edges.
Repeat rows 4–5, 3 times more.
Join in B and knit 2 rows in B (these 2 rows make the garter st ridge).
Continue alternating pattern as set and garter st ridges as follows:

- 6 rows A (as set)
- 2 rows B (ridge)
- 4 rows A (as set)
- 2 rows B (ridge)
- 12 rows A (as set)
- 2 rows B (ridge)
- 8 rows A (as set)
- 2 rows B (ridge)
- 4 rows A (as set)
- 2 rows B (ridge)

Change to A and knit 1 row, then work 3 rows seed st as rows 1–3.
Bind off in seed st.

DOG SQUARES
(MAKE 10 IN TOTAL)

With main color (mc), cast on 42 sts and work as for plain square, positioning dog as instructed below.

BORDER COLLIE

Work 3 rows seed st and then 10 rows st st with seed st edges.
Row 14: Seed st 3mc, k8mc, k2bl, k14mc, k3cr, k9mc, seed st 3mc.
Continue chart pattern (page 132) until dog is finished.
Work a further 10 rows in st st with seed st edges.
Work 3 rows seed st and bind off.

DALMATIAN (MAKE 2)

Work 3 rows seed st and then 8 rows st st with seed st edges.
Row 12: Seed st 3mc, k7mc, k2cr, k17mc, k2cr, k8mc, seed st 3mc.
Continue chart pattern (page 133) until dog is finished.
NOTE: The dog's tail will stop at the seed st edge.
Work a further 10 rows in st st with seed st edges.
Work 3 rows seed st and bind off.

JACK RUSSELL

Work 3 rows seed st and then
10 rows st st with seed st edges.
Row 14: Seed st 3mc, k5mc, k2cr,
k17mc, k2cr, k10mc, seed st 3mc.
Continue chart pattern (page 133)
until dog is finished.
Work a further 11 rows in st st with
seed st edges.
Work 3 rows seed st and bind off.

LABRADOR

Work as for Dalmatian using bl
instead of cr (same shape, no spots).
See page 134 for Labrador chart.

PUG (MAKE 2)

Work 3 rows seed st and then
10 rows st st with seed st edges.
Row 14: Seed st 3mc, k6mc, k3bl,
k12mc, k3bl, k12mc, seed st 3mc.
Continue chart pattern (page 134)
until dog is finished.
Work a further 7 rows in st st with
seed st edges.
Work 3 rows seed st and bind off.

WEST HIGHLAND TERRIER

Work 3 rows seed st and then
10 rows st st with seed st edges.
Row 14: Seed st 3mc, k4mc, k4mo,
k14mc, k3mo, k11mc, seed st 3mc.
Continue chart pattern (page 135)
until dog is finished.
Work a further 10 rows in st st with
seed st edges.
Work 3 rows seed st and bind off.

WHIPPET (MAKE 2)

Work 3 rows seed st and then
8 rows st st with seed st edges.
Row 12: Seed st 3mc, k6mc, k2cr,
k17mc, k2cr, k9mc, seed st 3mc.
Continue chart pattern (page 135)
until dog is finished.
Work a further 8 rows in st st with
seed st edges.
Work 3 rows seed st and bind off.

FINISHING

Using whipstitch, sew the squares
together as positioned on the blanket
plan (see page 119). Try to make
the seams as flat as possible. Add
finishing details if you wish, using
bl or me to sew 3-loop French knots
for eyes, cr to sew slanting stitches
above each of the Pug's eyes and
bl to make 1 duplicate stitch for
noses.

DALMATIAN
- Main color (mc) =
  Sea Fret (light grey – lg)
- Dog = Milk (cream – cr)
  and Pitch (black – bl)

**GARTER STITCH
RIDGE SQUARE**
- A = Milk (cream – cr)
- B = Iced Gem (aqua – ic)

LABRADOR
- Main color (mc) =
  Kanoko (pale blue – pb)
- Dog = Pitch (black – bl)

PLAIN SQUARE
- Mr Bhasin (petrol – mb)

STRIPED SQUARE
- A = Pretty
  (pale pink – pk)
- B = Milk (cream – cr)

JACK RUSSELL
- Main color (mc) =
  French (mauve – fr)
- Dog = Milk (cream cr)
  and Milk Chocolate (me)

STRIPED SQUARE
- A = Fawn (fn)
- B = Milk (cream – cr)

**WEST HIGHLAND
TERRIER**
- Main color (mc) = Pretty
  (pale pink – pk)
- Dog = Cream
  mohair (mo)

PUG
- Main color (mc) =
  Milk (cream – cr)
- Dog = Fawn (fn) and
  Pitch (black – bl)

PLAIN SQUARE
- Pretty (pale pink – pk)

WHIPPET
- Main color (mc) =
  Kanoko (pale blue – pb)
- Dog = Milk (cream – cr)
  and Mouse (grey – mu)

**GARTER STITCH
RIDGE SQUARE**
- A = Iced Gem (aqua – ic)
- B = Mr Bhasin
  (petrol – mb)

PLAIN SQUARE
- Sea Fret (light grey – lg)

BORDER COLLIE
- Main color (mc) =
  Iced Gem (aqua – ic)
- Dog = Pitch (black – bl)
  and Milk (cream – cr)

**GARTER STITCH
RIDGE SQUARE**
- A = Sea Fret
  (light grey – lg)
- B = Milk Chocolate (me)

DALMATIAN
- Main color (mc) =
  French (mauve – fr)
- Dog = Milk (cream – cr)
  and Pitch (black – bl)

WHIPPET
- Main color (mc) =
  Fawn (fn)
- Dog = Milk (cream – cr)
  and Mouse (grey – mu)

STRIPED SQUARE
- A = Mouse (grey – mu)
- B = Pretty
  (pale pink – pk)

PUG
- Main color (mc) =
  Mr Bhasin (petrol – mb)
- Dog = Fawn (fn) and
  Pitch (black – bl)

STRIPED SQUARE
- A = Fawn (fn)
- B = Kanoko
  (pale blue – pb)

ADULT SIZE

BEAGLE

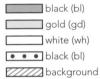

- black (bl)
- gold (gd)
- white (wh)
- black (bl)
- background

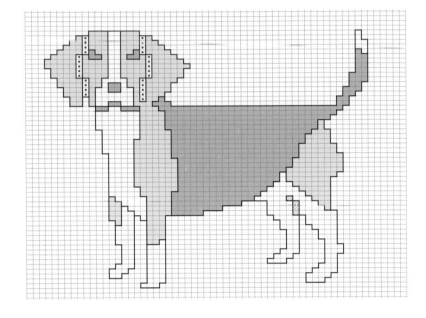

BORDER COLLIE

- black (bl)
- white (wh)
- background

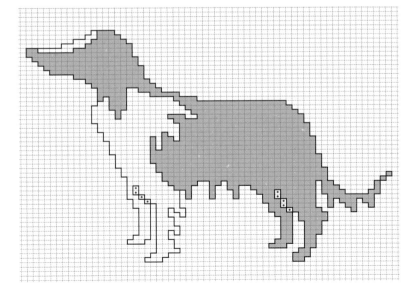

BORDER TERRIER

coffee (co)	
background	
charcoal (ch)	

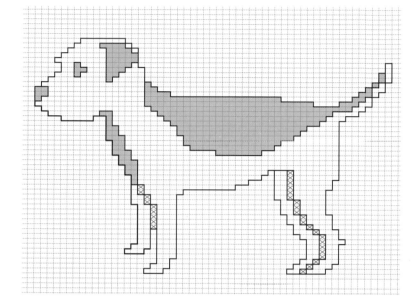

CHIHUAHUA

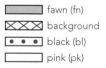

fawn (fn)	
background	
black (bl)	
pink (pk)	

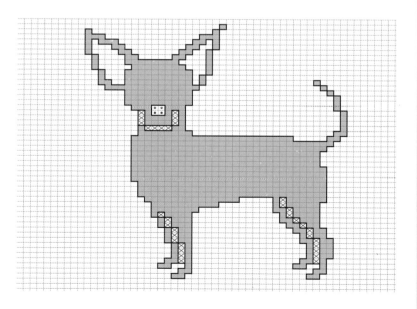

ADULT SIZE

DACHSHUND

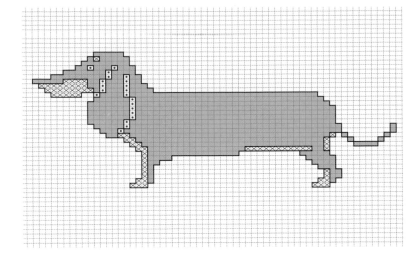

DALMATIAN

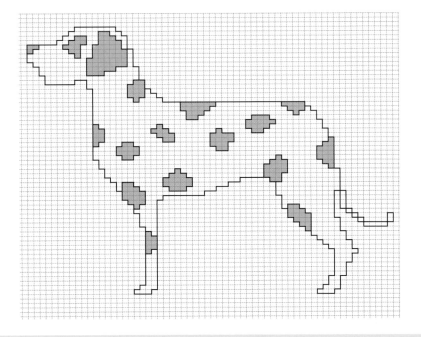

FRENCH BULLDOG

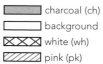 charcoal (ch)
background
white (wh)
pink (pk)

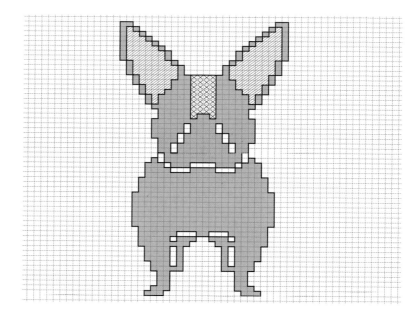

GOLDEN RETRIEVER

 fawn (fn)
black (bl)
background

ADULT SIZE

JACK RUSSELL

 cream (cr)

fawn (fn)

black (bl)

background

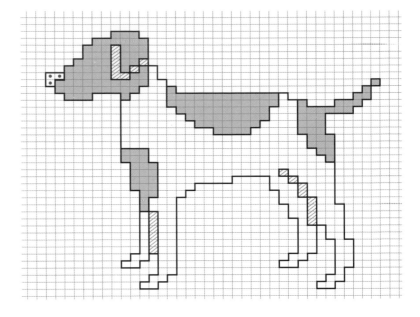

LABRADOODLE

white bouclé (ow)

background

black (bl)

NOTE: Swiss darn the eyes

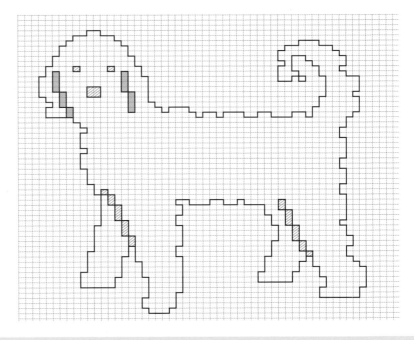

LABRADOR

▭ black (bl)

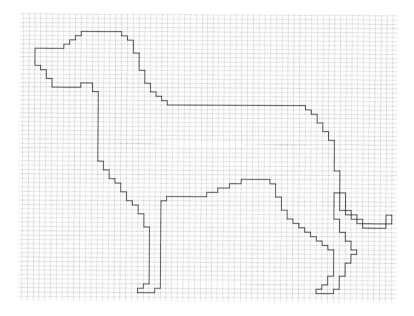

LURCHER

▭ 4 strands mohair (mo)
▭ • • • background
▨ charcoal (ch)

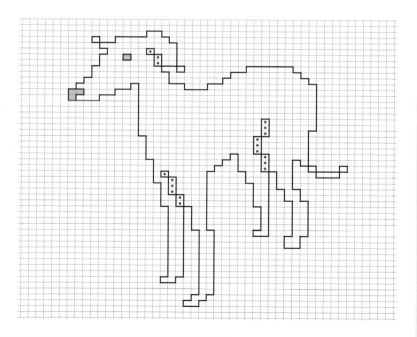

ADULT SIZE

MINIATURE SCHNAUZER

- ☐ 4 strands mohair (mo)
- ☒ background
- ▨ grey (gr)
- ▨ black (bl)
- ⦿ loopy stitch using 4 strands mohair (mo)

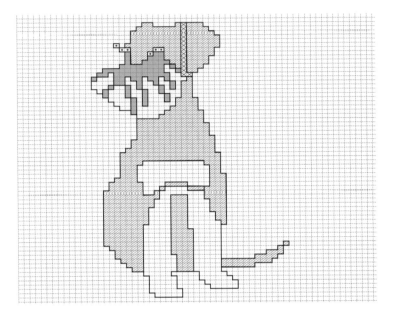

PUG

- ☐ oval color
- ☐ oatmeal (oa)
- ⦿ oval or background color
- ▨ charcoal (ch)

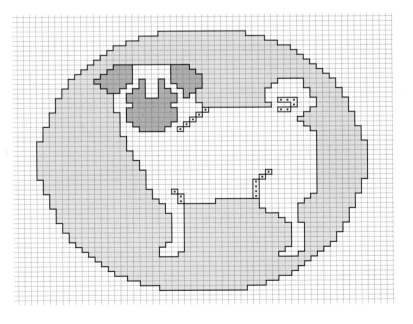

SPRINGER SPANIEL

- ▨ mahogany (ma)
- ▢ white (wh)
- ▧ black (bl)
- ▨ background

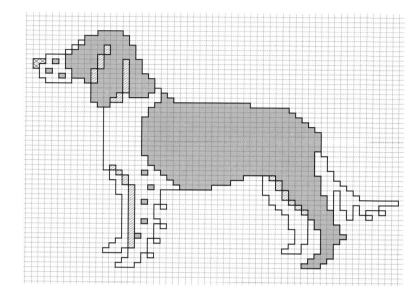

STAFFORDSHIRE
BULL TERRIER

- ▨ brown (br)
- ▢ white (wh)
- ⦿ background
- ▧ black (bl)

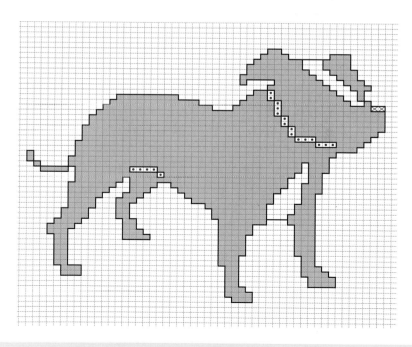

ADULT SIZE

WEST HIGHLAND TERRIER

☐	4 strands mohair (mo)
▨	black (bl)
⊠	pink (pk)

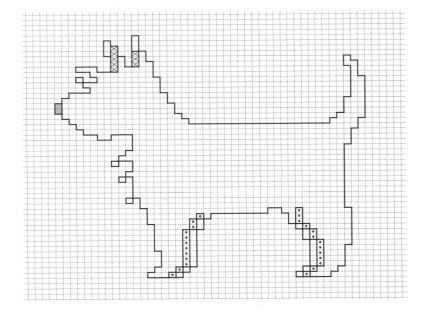

WHIPPET

☐	white (wh)
▨	background
▨	fawn (fn)
⊠	black (bl)

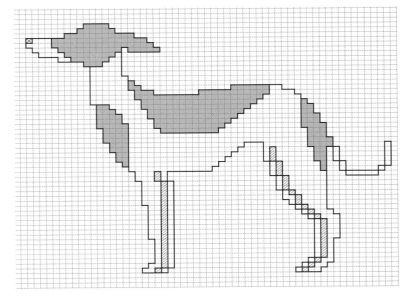

CAVE CANEM

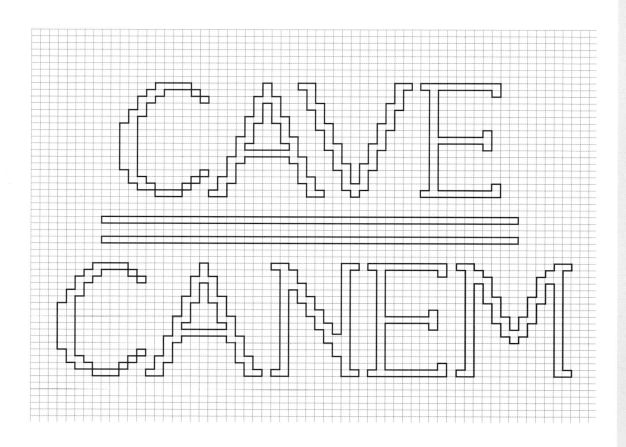

white (wh)

ALPHABET

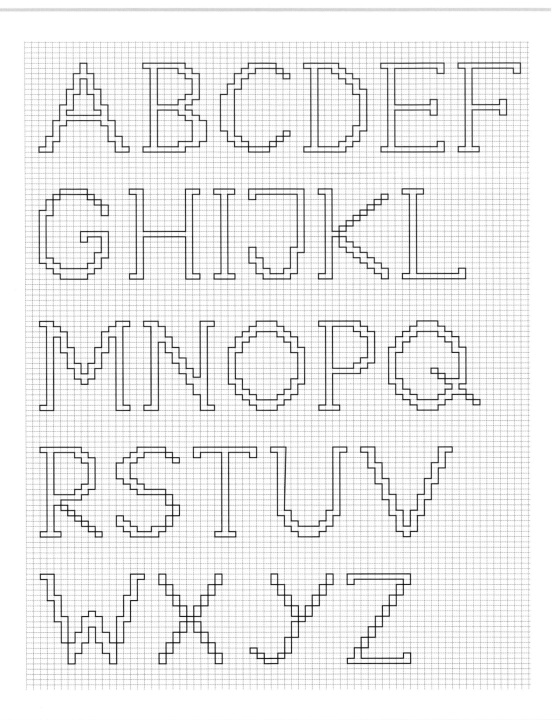

CHILD/BABY SIZE

BORDER COLLIE

 cream (cr)
black (bl)

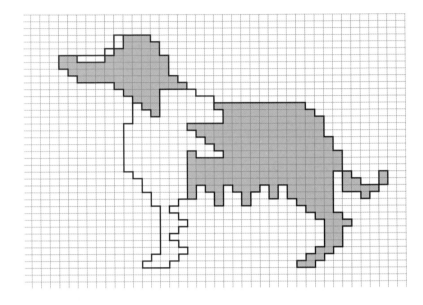

DACHSHUND

black (bl)
 ochre (oc)
• • • cream (cr)

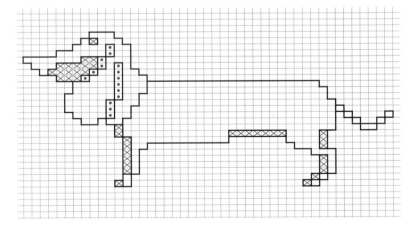

DALMATIAN

 cream (cr)
 black (bl)

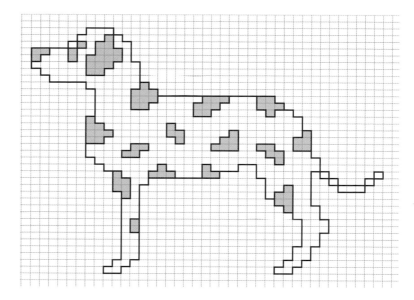

JACK RUSSELL

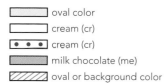 oval color
cream (cr)
• • • cream (cr)
milk chocolate (me)
oval or background color

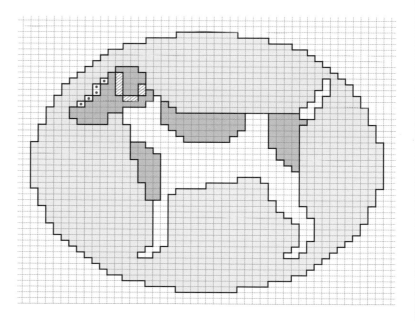

CHILD/BABY SIZE

LABRADOR

 black (bl)

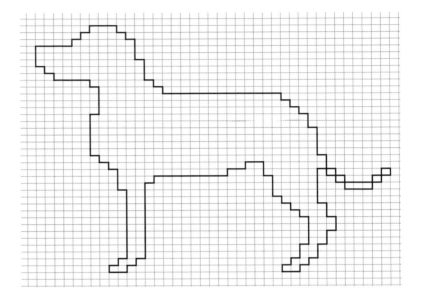

PUG

	fawn (fn)
• • •	background
	black (bl)

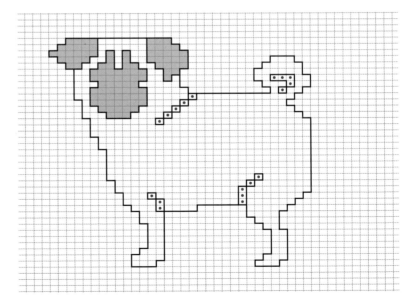

WEST HIGHLAND TERRIER

	3 strands mohair (mo)
⊠⊠⊠	black (bl)

NOTE: Make a duplicate stitch for the nose

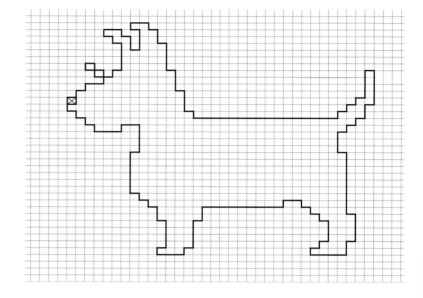

WHIPPET

	cream (cr)
▨	grey (mu)
⊠⊠⊠	black (bl)

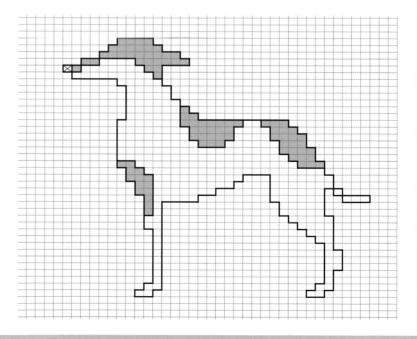

BABY'S CARDIGAN

JACK RUSSELL

 cream (cr)

milk chocolate (me)

cream (cr)

background

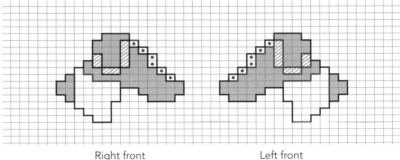

Right front   Left front

MINIATURE SCHNAUZER

3 strands mohair (mo)

background

grey (mu)

black (bl)

loopy stitch using 3 strands mohair (mo)

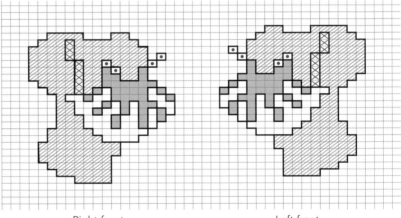

Right front   Left front

DACHSHUND

black (bl)

ochre (oc)

background

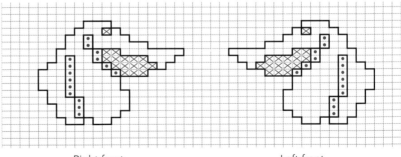

Right front   Left front

DALMATIAN ONESIE

CHART 1

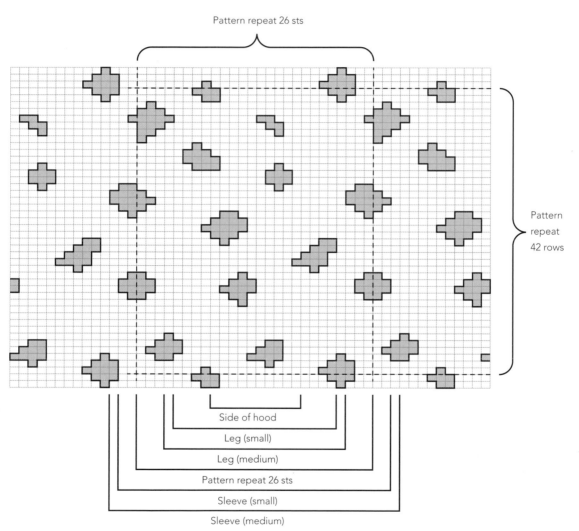

Pattern repeat 26 sts

Pattern repeat 42 rows

Side of hood

Leg (small)

Leg (medium)

Pattern repeat 26 sts

Sleeve (small)

Sleeve (medium)

DALMATIAN ONESIE

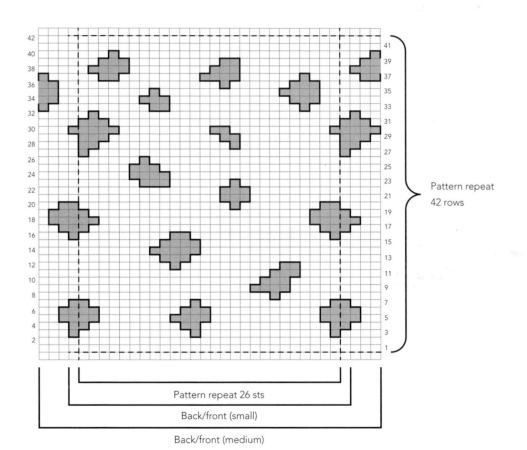

Pattern repeat
42 rows

Pattern repeat 26 sts

Back/front (small)

Back/front (medium)

INDEX OF DOGS

Adult sizes	Width	Height	Yarn and instructions	Chart
Beagle	51 sts	54 rows	page 32	page 120
Border Collie	62 sts	52 rows	page 58	page 120
Border Terrier	55 sts	48 rows	page 56	page 121
Cave Canem	58 sts	44 rows	page 64	page 129
Chihuahua	39 sts	50 rows	page 42	page 121
Dachshund	60 sts	30 rows	page 62	page 122
Dalmatian	62 sts	60 rows	page 34	page 122
French Bulldog	26 sts	56 rows	page 38	page 123
Golden Retriever	65 sts	56 rows	page 40	page 123
Jack Russell	36 sts	37 rows	page 50	page 124
Labradoodle	48 sts	55 rows	page 48	page 124
Labrador	62 sts	60 rows	page 28	page 125
Lurcher	36 sts	47 rows	page 30	page 125
Miniature Schnauzer	35 sts	65 rows	page 52	page 126
Pug	35 sts	40 rows	page 36	page 126
Springer Spaniel	57 sts	49 rows	page 44	page 127
Staffordshire Bull Terrier	52 sts	49 rows	page 46	page 127
West Highland Terrier	44 sts	46 rows	page 60	page 128
Whippet	57 sts	52 rows	page 54	page 128

Child/baby sizes	Width	Height	Yarn and instructions	Chart
Border Collie	36 sts	34 rows	page 90	page 132
Dachshund	46 sts	25 rows	page 86	page 132
Dalmatian	39 sts	36 rows	page 82	page 133
Jack Russell	34 sts	33 rows	page 92	page 133
Labrador	39 sts	36 rows	page 84	page 134
Pug	32 sts	37 rows	page 88	page 134
West Highland Terrier	34 sts	34 rows	page 80	page 135
Whippet	34 sts	38 rows	page 94	page 135

Additional chart designs	Width	Height	Yarn and instructions	Chart
Alphabet	–	17 rows	page 64	page 130
Baby's cardigan	–	–	page 72	page 136
Dalmatian onesie	–	–	page 102	pages 137, 138

ABBREVIATIONS

approx	approximately	**oz**	ounce(s)
beg	begin(ning)	**p**	purl
cm	centimeter(s)	**p2tog**	purl next two stitches together
dec	knit (purl) two stitches together to decrease by one stitch	**rem**	remain(ing)
g	gram(s)	**rep**	repeat
in	inch(es)	**RS**	right side
inc	work in the front and back of next stitch to increase by one stitch	**st(s)**	stitch(es)
k	knit	**st st**	stockinette stitch
k2tog	knit next two stitches together	**WS**	wrong side
m1	from the front, use tip of left needle to pick up horizontal strand of yarn between last stitch worked and next stitch, then knit through back of it to make one stitch	**yo**	yarn over
		[ ]	square brackets either contain instructions or information relating to larger sizes in multiple-size patterns, or indicate instructions to be worked as directed after the closing bracket
mm	millimeter(s)	*****	work instructions after asterisk(s) as directed

RESOURCES

Cascade Yarn is widely, available in local yarn stores or online from:
- www.yarn.com
- www.loveknitting.com/us
- www.cascadeyarns.com

Erika Knight, Debbie Bliss and Rowan yarns are available from most local yarn stores or online from:
- www.yarn.com
- www.loveknitting.com/us
- www.jimmybeanswool.com

Drops Alpaca Bouclé yarn is available from:
- www.woolwarehouse.co.uk

If you are unable to obtain any of the yarn used in this book, it can be replaced with a yarn of a similar weight and composition. Please note, the finished projects may vary slightly from those shown, depending on the yarn used. Try Yarnsub.com for suggestions.

For more information on selecting or substituting yarn, contact your local yarn shop or an online store; they are familiar with all types of yarns and would be happy to help you. Additionally, the online knitting community at Ravelry.com has forums where you can post questions about specific yarns.

PHOTOGRAPHY CREDITS

Ursula Aitchison of Phodography:
Cover photography and images on pages 4, 7, 11, 12, 13, 14, 17, 19, 21, 29, 31, 33, 35, 37, 39, 41, 43, 45, 47, 49, 51, 53, 55, 57, 59, 61, 63, 65, 66, 69, 71, 73 (top right), 73 (bottom right), 81, 83, 85, 87, 89, 91, 93, 95, 96, 100, 103, 107, 109, 113, 115, 131, 139, 142 and 144.

Martin Norris: images on pages 22, 23, 24, 25, 26, 27, 73 (left), 76, 77, 78, 79, 98, 99, 110, 111 and 118.

ACKNOWLEDGEMENTS

Many people have been involved in the making of this book and we would like to profusely thank Krissy Mallett for her endless encouragement, calming nature and spreadsheet skills; Katie Cowan for loyally commissioning this book; Michelle Pickering for editing the book into shape; Marilyn Wilson for her brilliant forensic pattern checking; Michelle Mac and Sophie Yamamoto for working magic with the design; Kuo Kang Chen for drawing our charts so brilliantly; Martin Norris for his attention to detail; Lindsey Poole for the beautiful make-up and hair; and the wonderful Ursula Aitchison of Phodography for her glorious lifestyle photography and excellent dog whispering skills (www.phodography.org.uk).

A huge thank you to Cascade in the US and Erika Knight in the UK for their amazing yarns and generosity in supporting this book.

Thank you too to our understanding and expert knitters, Deidre, Sheila, Lyn, Rosemary, Sylvia and her team.

We have asked and cajoled quite a few friends and friends of friends to model the knitwear and bring along their wonderful dogs, so a huge thank you must go to: Abigail, Albert, Audrey, Audrey B, Bella, Beth, Betsy, Caitlin, Caroline, Cilla, Clover, Daisy, Daniel B, Daniel T, Dougal, Dylan, Eliza, Elsie, Ember, Etienne, Felix, Figgie, Florence C, Florence K, Francesca, Fred, Frida, Gracie, Gregory, Henry, Herbie, Huxley, Jeremy, Jessica B, Jessica E, Jo, Junior, Katherine, Katy, Kelly, Kim, Laurie, Louise G, Louise P, Lucky, Maude, Maxx, Michael, Mick, Mike, Millie, Molly, Morgan, Oscar, Oscar M-H, Patrick, Pegasus, Percy, Peter, Phoenix, Poppy, Ramona, Rooney, Siobhan, Spice, Stanley, Steph, Susan, Suzanna, Ted, Theo, Wilfred, Winnie, Zoe, Zoe L and, of course, the remarkable Hugo.

Sally Muir and Joanna Osborne are co-authors of the bestselling *Best in Show* series of knitting books. This is their tenth book and combines their two great interests: knitting and dogs. They have run their own knitwear business, Muir and Osborne, for many years, exporting to stores in the United States, Japan and Europe as well as selling to shops in the United Kingdom. Several pieces of their knitwear are in the permanent collection at the Victoria and Albert Museum, London, including their red sheep sweater as worn by Princess Diana.

To see the books and current collection, go to www.muirandosborne.co.uk or follow us on Instagram @muirandosborne